Winner, Dog Writers Association of America 2025 Writing Competition, Memoir

"This book is a celebration of the indelible bond between humans and their four-legged 'teachers.' A must-read for dog lovers and seekers of spiritual growth alike."
—Fran Weil, Pet Chaplain,
 The Perfect Paws Pet Ministry

"With a remarkably open heart, author Ellen Finnie reveals the magic and the essential gold of the human-dog relationship, the numerous gems of spiritual connection any dog owner is sure to understand... a delightful, poignant, and enlightening look directly into the eyes of these beloved spirit animals with a sense of hope and wonder."
—David W. Berner, best-selling author of
 Walks with Sam and *Daylight Saving Time*

"*The Ten Perfections* is a perfect tribute to the many gifts our pets give us—love, compassion, loyalty, empathy—and the monumental ways they shape our lives, even decades after they're gone. Fans of Sy Montgomery's *How to Be a Good Creature* and Jennifer Finney Boylan's *Good Boy: My Life in Seven Dogs* will love Finnie's moving memoir!"
—E.B. Bartels, author of *Good Grief: On Loving Pets, Here and Hereafter*

the TEN PERFECTIONS

*Spiritual Lessons
from a Life with Dogs*

ELLEN FINNIE

Connect with the author at
ellenfinnie.substack.com

The Ten Perfections:
Spiritual Lessons from a Life with Dogs

ISBN 979-8-9928655-1-6 (paperback)
ISBN 979-8-9928655-0-9 (eBook)
Library of Congress Control Number: 2025906138

Photos of Isabel and Gracie by Susanne Personette
Publication managed by AuthorImprints.com

Publisher's Cataloging-in-Publication (Provided by Cassidy Cataloguing Services, Inc.)
Names: Finnie, Ellen, author.
Title: The ten perfections : spiritual lessons from a life with dogs / Ellen Finnie.
Description: Arlington, Massachusetts : Canid Heart Publishing, [2025] | Includes bibliographical references.
Identifiers: LCCN: 2025906138 | ISBN: 9798992865516 (paperback) | 9798992865509 (ebook)
Subjects: LCSH: Finnie, Ellen. | Dog owners--Biography. | Human-animal relationships. | Buddhism. | Dogs--Religious aspects. | LCGFT: Autobiographies. | BISAC: PETS / Essays & Narratives. | PETS / Dogs / General. | BIOGRAPHY & AUTOBIOGRAPHY / Memoirs.
Classification: LCC: SF422.82.F56 A3 2025 | DDC: 636.70092--dc23

To my beloved parents,
Bruce and Ginnie Finnie, whose love, belief, and
generosity have been precious, unceasing gifts.

To my daughter Nat, who taught me what love is.

To my partner Jaime, who fills my life
with love, joy, adventure, and peace.

And to all dogs, everywhere,
and the people who love them—

Love, Always

CONTENTS

A NOTE ON THIS WORK OF MEMORY

These stories are a product of my mutable and imperfect memory. In writing this book I have dedicated myself to being truthful, but the passage of time and my own limited perspective have inevitably shaped every memory I have, in ways I cannot know. This is especially the case for some earlier events, where I have had to rebuild from fragments of memory. So I share these stories not as an unerring transcript of my life, but as my best effort at representing it truthfully, through recalling and reconstructing it. Names have been changed to protect privacy.

PREFACE

My young Golden retriever Leo and I are sitting together on the rug in the school counselor's office, waiting and watching for a particular student, one of Leo's favorite friends. The rug, like the room, invites calm. It is decorated with a scene of a small pond, bursting with lily pads and frogs, its shores linked by a fanciful wooden bridge. I've chosen to sit on the bridge, the place where our connections begin. As the student comes through the door, her round face lights up, a miniature sun warming the room.

"Leo! My Floof!" she calls, with her special nickname for Leo.

This young girl knows Leo well. We have been visiting as a therapy dog team for many months. Leo's presence offers the elementary school students relief from academic or social challenges, or any extra burdens they carry.

As soon as he sees her, Leo gets up to greet the girl, his tail wagging softly, his face relaxed, his mouth loosely open—a doggie smile. He rubs one of his long, broad sides and then the other back and forth against her, and begins a quiet but high-pitched cry, his song of joy, reserved for greeting his special people. The girl's small hands move with sureness across his back, caressing him with her strong fingers, thrust deep into his thick, creamy coat. Leo leans a bit towards the girl as she massages him, and his voice changes from his greeting song to a low moan of pleasure. She smiles.

"I've waited all day to see you! Wanna go to the playhouse?"

They walk side by side, the girl's hand on Leo's back, and tuck themselves together in the small structure. It is a cozy retreat for children in the counselor's office, a tiny house full of pillows, its doorway lined with miniature stuffed squirrels, owls, and other woodland creatures. The girl perches on the small chair, Leo at her feet, and she pets him rhythmically. Leo lies on a quilt, places his head on his paws, his eyes partially closed.

Their peace and joy—their ease and happiness together—are a force-field, and I am pulled in. We sit, the girl's hands on Leo, her face glowing, her eyes bright.

She leans forward to kiss Leo's massive head, and murmurs "I love you, Leo."

The moments in this room are simple, and brief. And yet they are a brimming cup of what matters most in life: Love, joy, connection. Every time I am I in that force-field, I feel gratitude and wonder at how the shared joy in these simple moments can be as meaningful as anything life—even a very fortunate life, like mine —delivers. This bounty is possible because of Leo.

Leo, the loving source of all the joy and ease. Leo, here with me in this room, is the miracle. Our moments are a simple but full expression of the magic that dogs can heal, and help us find happiness. His gift is to offer his love, purely, and avidly, without asking for anything but connection. His gift is to transmit love so genuinely through his soft almond eyes that his gaze warms your bones and opens your heart.

And yet our presence together in this room is not only about Leo. It is a culmination of my own growth, growth through partnership with Leo—and with all my dogs. Through them and their qualities of heart, I have found joy, and peace, and, at last, my calling.

It has not been a direct route to reach this point. Leo, here by the student's side, calmly connected, is the same Leo whose wild, intense hunting drive, whose eager energy and excitement, are such vital forces that friends gently observed they could not see him ever being a therapy dog, and perhaps might do better on a farm. How the wild and wonderful Leo and I made our way into this little room is a story—one story from a long passage of over sixty years, a continuous, unending journey of growing and learning from my beloved dogs.

I share these stories of Leo, and all the dogs that came before him, in gratitude for all they've taught, and all they've given. And I share these stories as my small tribute to the love and happiness that people and dogs, through their ancient, powerful bond, find together.

NOTE TO READER

When my mother was asked to write about what characterized each of her children most fully, she reported just one thing about me: "Ellen always loved dogs." From my earliest years, I've shared my life with my dogs, and they have brought profound blessings. Their love has brought me safely off a mountaintop in a blinding storm and across a marathon finish line; their open hearts have connected me to others in ways I couldn't manage on my own, including finding me true and lasting love. Their companionship has supported me through every one of life's difficulties, helping me navigate a circuitous career path, a failed marriage, health challenges, and my self-made demons too. Living with them has brought me to dig deeper for compassion and understanding and to find the peace of no secrets.

All my dogs have encouraged me in their own ways to develop what are described in Buddhist teachings as "qualities of the heart," or the Ten Perfections: Generosity, Morality, Renunciation, Wisdom, Energy, Patience, Truthfulness, Determination, Lovingkindness, and Equanimity. These "Perfections" are not intended as a path to perfection or even to self-improvement. They offer a different kind of path—a path of kindness, which in turn yields happiness. Happiness for ourselves, and through us, for others. The promise of the teachings is that by developing and expressing these qualities of the heart, we can become less weighed down by suffering, less burdened by shame and judgment, and more loving and open to others and the world. We become happier.

I am not a Buddhist scholar or teacher, and I am in no way an expert in these teachings. I came across them at a time of crisis in my life when my daughter was struggling in school and was being tested for learning disabilities. Nothing I could do seemed to help, and the pressure of trying to do the right thing merely revealed my powerlessness in the face her heart-wrenching difficulties; it made me feel my mind was breaking apart into shards of glass. Desperate for some way to pull the fragments into a focused whole, to reach something I vaguely thought of as mindfulness, I found these teachings in a book by Sylvia Boorstein, *Pay Attention for Goodness' Sake: Practicing the Perfections of the Heart—The Buddhist Path to Kindness.* And with them, I found a different way to approach life: not as an endless, linear climb towards some arbitrary vision of success but as a path of the heart, a path of kindness, focused on being present for life as it really is. A path that can lead to internal peace and happiness.

My dogs helped me along this path. These stories are about how my partnership with them has encouraged me to develop these heart qualities as I interpret and understand them, not as an expert, but as a fellow traveler on life's journey. Their perfections have been my practice, a lifelong effort to let kindness in and to let it lead me—and, I hope, lead my beloved dogs and the people near and dear to me—to lead all of us to happiness. It's not a journey that concludes, not a point of perfection to reach and hold onto. It's a journey of getting up every day, looking into the face of these beings who are so loving, so attached, so trusting, so open, and bowing with gratitude for the unearned grace of heading out for another walk together.

And so I share these stories to celebrate, thank, and honor my beloved dogs and to commit to trying to be worthy of them. Not only do they reflect the Ten Perfections—they *are* my Ten Perfections.

1

YANKEE – MORALITY

The bliss of blamelessness

My neighborhood friends called to me as I made my way on the short path between our houses. They were engrossed in a game of TV tag, guessing the names of television shows from initials scratched in the dirt, sprinting off when they cracked the code. I liked that game, but today I had something more important to do. I called out "Gotta go!" and kept on towards the sidewalk along the busy street. I felt for the lump in my pocket, where I'd put the money my grandmother had given me for my birthday.

Today was the day. My Puppy was waiting for me.

My world as a child was roughly bounded by the train tracks at the far side of a field; the road, thrumming with traffic; the woods behind our small neighborhood houses; and as far up the hill as the swing set behind my friend's house at the top of Rockaway Lane—the one with rusty metal legs dug just a little into the ground, chains holding three plastic seats, where we liked to sit and beat our legs back and forth, our knees pumping hard, the effort sending us soaring up into the sky. But now that I was eight, I could go way past the swing set. I was allowed to walk across the street or up the road to the shops, as long as I got home when called for dinner. I would hear my mother's voice singing out into the gathering dusk and would trot back down the hill to our house. But today she wouldn't be calling any time soon. I had plenty of time before dinner.

It was a warm afternoon for November in New England. The grey clouds were soft and close, holding my secret. I passed the edge of the athletic field and turned up toward the Heights, where I often visited the five-and-dime store, the library, and the church—the one with the crisp white paint, bright red wooden doors, and a tall steeple pointing up so high into the silver sky that it almost lifted me too. These were all important places for me, but the Heights also held my most favorite place—the pet store.

I walked past my neighbor's house and thought how much their dog, Pal, the cocker spaniel who had become my friend, would like to come with me on this trip. He could help me find a puppy just like him—with his shiny black coat and long wavy ears, his huge round brown eyes, and his short wiggling tail. Whenever I knocked at Pal's house, his people would smile, grab his leash, and hold it out to me. Then Pal and I would be on our way. He was my special buddy, a partner for trips into the woods, to Eagle Rock, and across the road to the hidden swamp behind the gas station, where we looked for tadpoles together. When I was with Pal, everything felt right.

But I could not take Pal with me today.

A slight shiver went through me, even though I wore a light jacket and my favorite shirt, my brother's old plaid flannel. I started walking faster, past the houses where my friends lived, past the old tracks where we'd leave our pennies to be crushed by the trains, and past the church, where I went to Sunday school. My family didn't go to church anymore, but all the other kids in the neighborhood did, and I had asked my mom if I could go. She said I could if I wanted to. Just this past week, we had read a story from the Bible about people surviving a fire in a huge furnace. I felt funny reading that story. It didn't make sense to me. Nothing like that happened in my world. I didn't even see magic like that on my favorite show, *Lost in Space,* where Will Robinson and his astronaut family lived through so many unexpected things in every single episode. But I knew how the teacher would want me to answer the questions in the Sunday school workbook, and sure enough, I got all gold stars. It didn't feel as good as I thought it would. But maybe if I kept at it, I'd be more like the other kids, the ones who seemed to share things I didn't understand.

But My Puppy would not care about any of that.

I quickened my step and kept on, glancing at the house with that perfect bike propped outside, the one with the banana seat and butterfly handlebars, colored streamers attached. I could use the money in my pocket for a bike like that, or even for the cowgirl boots I dreamed of. I would love to be a cowgirl, flying on horseback, free. But there wasn't any doubt in my mind. This money was for a puppy. I didn't need that bike or those boots like I needed a puppy. My Puppy.

My feet were now fast and sure, nothing holding me back, not even the requirement that I be polite to Mrs. O'Leary, who met my brother and sister and me at our house after school on days like today when my mother was off at night school in the city. I could picture the scrambled eggs Mrs. O'Leary had made today, with the yucky white specks in them. I had left most of them on my plate. It was so good not to be looking at those eggs or at Mrs. O'Leary's expectant face.

At the corner light, where the Heights began, I looked across to Mr. Baruch's store, the one where I'd bought the ceramic statue of the boxer and her puppies with the money I stole from my brother's coin collection, popping the dimes and nickels out from the cardboard display. I felt a bit queasy thinking about that, just like when I looked at Mrs. O'Leary's eggs.

I crossed at the light, looking up the hill, my eyes on the sign for the pet store. I ran the last few steps and pulled open the door. As I burst into the familiar, narrow dark space, the bell rang, as always, announcing my presence to the man behind the counter. He looked up from his magazine. He didn't exactly smile, but he didn't look mean. I clenched my fist tight in my pocket around my money, my chest still heaving from my sprint up the hill. I tried to keep from gulping air, pretending interest in the guinea pigs darting around in their cage, stirring up the sweet smell of cedar shavings, and the parakeets chattering from their perches along the wall. I glanced sideways towards the back of the store.

There they were, eight wriggling puppies in a big box. All black. Like Pal. I walked slowly down the aisle and bent over them as I had when I'd visited the week before. But today was different. One of these puppies was My Puppy. He'd be by my side, my best friend, just like Pal.

The man came out from behind the register and stood near me as I looked at the puppies.

"Can I help you?" he asked. Today he seemed enormous, towering over me, his huge eyes peering at me from under tousled hair.

I froze. *Maybe I should just ask about food for my guinea pigs.* But I looked down again at the puppies, now climbing over each other in the excitement of people nearby, and told him quietly, "I want a puppy."

"You mean you want to buy a puppy?"

I quickly pulled the money out of my pocket where he could see it. He had to know I could pay.

"Yes, I have my money."

"Perhaps you'd like to hold this one," he said, choosing the largest puppy, who had his paws on the edge of the box, scrabbling at the side. He placed the puppy in my arms. Warmth surged through me. I held him close as he wriggled, his fur shiny black, his tail a tiny whip of joy, his floppy ears hanging so low they laid upon my arm.

"He's a good one, the biggest boy in the litter. He'll be the size of a cocker spaniel," the man offered. *Like Pal,* I thought. *But mine, just mine.*

I buried my face in the puppy's warm fur, my voice muffled. "I can take him now?"

"He's ready to go," the man said. "How about a collar and leash for him?" He grabbed a slim red collar and a silver chain leash, clipping both to the puppy and draping the leash across my shoulder. Then he turned and made his way back to the counter. I followed him, carrying the puppy, not daring to breathe.

Behind the register, the man paused. I stood before him, the puppy in my arms. My stomach felt strange, like when I'd given the man at Baruch's five-and-dime my brother's special coins.

"Ten dollars please," he said.

I put the puppy down and dug for my cash, holding it out over the counter.

"Your parents okay with it?" he asked, kind of quickly, as he took the money.

I was ready. "My parents love puppies. He's for my birthday."

It wasn't quite a lie.

I held the leash, looking down at the puppy sniffing and darting, happy with his freedom outside the cardboard box but twisting a bit against the unfamiliar constraints of the chain. One of my hands went to my stomach, Mrs. O'Leary's icky eggs churning in my gut. The puppy pulled and jumped, the parakeets shrieked, and guinea pigs took up the chorus with their high-pitched squeaks and squeals.

"Well okay, then. Hope you enjoy him, kid!"

I didn't wait for him to say more—I picked up My Puppy and strode to the door, the bell sounding sharply, like an alarm, as I fled. My Puppy at my heels, I ran down the sidewalk, feeling just like I did when I swung so high on the swing set on Rockaway Lane that the thin metal legs pulled right up out of the earth on each forward pass of the swing. I felt that same terrifying, glorious sensation that was like flying, and just a bit like falling too.

When I walked into our small house along with My Puppy, I braced myself for a strong reaction from my parents. But my father surprised me. He put his hands on My Puppy's round head, stroking his long ears. Looking into his huge eyes, he said, "If we keep him, we'll call him Yankee."

Yankee didn't turn out to be the size of a cocker; he was like an oversized version of the retriever in my dog book, with long wavy ears and fur and the solid muscles and wild eagerness of a young sporting dog. He seemed so happy as we explored the wonders of our world together—the squirrels, the trees, my neighborhood friends. His tongue would hang loose, as if he had forgotten to attend to it with so many sights and sounds to enjoy. When I caught his gaze, his brown eyes shone, pools emitting their own light. With him next to me, I was home.

But as the days shortened, and Yankee got bigger and bigger, I began to feel smaller and smaller. One cold day after school, when we were out together, Yankee saw a squirrel and took off into the woods with me attached to his leash. I fell into the leaves, and he dragged me along the ground. The squirrel escaped up a tree, and Yankee leapt and whined and scrabbled at the bark. I lay on the ground, the leash still wound around my hand. I was scratched, stinging, and covered in dirt and leaves.

After the squirrel disappeared, Yankee seemed to notice me again and jumped gleefully back and forth over me, licking my face. We made our way back to the house, Yankee bounding with excitement. But my shoulders were slumped. I'd read *The Rin Tin Tin Book of Dog Care* many times, borrowing it over and over from the library, and I could tell that Yankee wasn't acting at all like the striking German Shepherd on the cover, who posed calmly and had clearly learned to "heel," "sit," and "stay" just as the book explained. Yankee wasn't anything like that dog, and certainly not like Rin Tin Tin, the famously well-trained movie-star dog. Yankee wasn't even like my calm and quiet buddy, Pal.

Then one evening as fall was turning towards winter, when my dad was grilling a steak in our backyard, Yankee lunged and grabbed the entire hunk of meat right off the charcoal fire. My dad shouted and began running after Yankee. The steak was meant as dinner for all five of us, but Yankee was too fast for him and managed to consume the whole thing before my father caught him. The dog was alight and wriggling with his unexpected treat, his mouth open, eyes sparkling. My dad's lips were in a tight line, his jaw taut, as he led Yankee by the collar back into the house.

Whether it was my being pulled down so many times, or whether it was the steak, not long after that, my parents told me Yankee needed a new home, a better place for him, where he could run and play. I lay awake in the night, trying to picture the place My Puppy would live. Fields? Woods? A farm? Someplace where he could run free all day. I tried to believe it would be better for him, like my parents said. But as I lay in bed in a crumpled ball, the sheets pulled over my head, my whole body hurt. I didn't cry. I knew the truth: I had begun my life with Yankee in a lie, and then I had failed him completely. I had gone to get my puppy all on my own, and my father had let me keep him. But I had failed in my responsibility to care for him and train him. Even with all I'd read, I could not find a way to get Yankee to walk on a leash without him pulling me down or to keep him from stealing steaks and running wild. I had failed him and lost him as a result. There was no one to blame but myself. I did not deserve to grieve.

———

Many years later, I came to understand why my father had let me keep Yankee, for a time, even though I'd acquired him without permission. My father's life back then was overflowing with demands and commitments. He had three young children and was building his career. We had other pets—guinea pigs and cats. Most fathers in this situation would have said no to more pets. But what I came to see decades later, as an adult and a parent myself, is that when I was eight and walked through the door with My Puppy, what my father saw in the face of the long-eared pup with the wide, soulful eyes was his *own* Yankee—the dog who had come into his life at about the same age I was back then.

At ten years old, my father's future had been laid out like a smooth road before him, his name already painted with pride on the door of his father's roofing company: "Bruce Finnie and Son" carefully rendered. But on one otherwise unremarkable day, his father was suddenly taken to the hospital and never came home. He died under mysterious circumstances that my father never understood. What my dad did know was that after his father died, he was "lost and alone." The familiar heat of the Memphis sun, which had warmed him when he and his father fished in a small rowboat in the Mississippi river delta, was suddenly swept away. That safe and comfortable world was replaced by the alien gray chill of a Midwestern winter, where his mother—now a widow, though only in her thirties—had retreated to her childhood home. Awash in grief, she moved my young father and his sister, Sallie, to live with their grandparents, and tried to build a new life.

My dad would speak of that time only when asked, and only much later in his life. But when he did, he invariably mentioned his Yankee. "Yankee brought me joy in the darkest time of my life," he told me, his voice reverent, quiet. When he spoke of Yankee, his voice always softened that way, and his eyes, especially if he had a glass of whiskey in his hand, would mist over a bit. One time he told me that "Yankee mattered so much to my sister, and she was so alone after our father died. She had no one. My mother was distracted by her grief, and I couldn't be there for Sallie. But Yankee was. Yankee was such a comfort to her."

Because of the way my father talked of Yankee, and the rarity of his reflections, Yankee became a kind of mystical creature in my own mind until, deep into my own middle age, I found a single picture of him, tucked into a pile of unsorted photographs that had come to my father after his mother's death. The photo drew Yankee out of myth and into reality: I looked down at the photo in my hand and saw him, a handsome brown and white spaniel with long floppy ears and a wavy coat. Across the better part of a century, I was held in the presence of this dog, this dog who meant so much to my father. There was Yankee, sitting loyally at the side of my father's sister, Sallie. His sincere brown eyes were attentive, as if he were still sharing his vigilant, wise, and loving care.

My dad was not much for using words like "love" or offering up how he felt about things. But I see now, after his death, that whether he knew it or not, when he spoke of his childhood dog and his sister, he was telling me as much about what Yankee meant to him as to Sallie. I can see so clearly now that the day I walked into our house with a puppy I'd bought without permission, my father wanted me to have the lasting love he'd had with his Yankee. He wanted me to have my own Yankee, my own friend and supporter. That wish he had for me was more important to him than my transgression.

———

When my father lay in a hospital bed at the end of his long life, in what turned out to be his final hours, the confusion caused by his failing kidneys briefly lifted. And when he found the energy to speak, it was of his most seminal memories. With his mind turned to the deepest, most core, most significant relationships of his life, he spoke of Yankee.

"Yankee was a hero for me. He got me through my father's death. He was always there for us."

As he was dying, my dad was at last able to say it: "I loved him."

Despite the profound and devastating loss of his father when he was only ten, my father's final message to me was not how easily you can lose love, but how it lasts. Nearly eighty years after his Yankee stood by his side, my father's life now laid out behind him, he was once again held in the warmth and love and protection of that good dog—a dear, trusted companion to lean on in his final journey.

My generous father never faulted me for seeking that kind of love with my own Yankee. I managed that, all on my own. My selfish action, and its results, have haunted me. I have been tormented through the years by recurrent night terrors, bursting out of sleep into the horror that I have let a puppy die by forgetting to feed him or give him medication or by mistakenly leaving him abandoned in a vacation house without food or water. In the first moments of these terrors, the torment of having caused the painful death of an innocent and deeply beloved creature due to my own failures rips through me as if my soul is being sliced out of me with a burning saber. The psychic agony of those moments is a sharp dive into hell. Inconsolable, frantic, despairing, and desperate, I scream. I writhe.

And then, some small part of my brain tries to save me, to draw me out of the crushing anguish, to begin to believe that perhaps, just perhaps, I didn't kill a puppy. At least not that night.

I don't know for certain whether these recurrent terrors stem from what happened with Yankee, but I believe there's a connection. I crossed a moral line as a young child and did something selfish and reckless that involved another being. I wanted a puppy, and without consulting anyone, I got myself a puppy. I was only eight, but somewhere in me, I knew this was out of bounds. I let myself be blinded by my own needs and desires, and I told myself I was prepared to take care of Yankee, but I wasn't.

I have come to understand the reverberation of my actions through the lens of Buddhist teachings. In Buddhism, morality can be described as a practice of five precepts. The first of these in some sense encompasses the others, as all five precepts are different ways to say "I'll do no harm."[1] The first precept, like the others, is simple: "I vow to abstain from harming living beings." This vow, as with practicing each of the Perfections, is seen as a path not to self-improvement or even to noble altruism, but to happiness. The personal payoff of doing no harm is "the bliss of blamelessness." I've been seeking that bliss since I was eight, when I felt the double torment of harming Yankee, my dear, cherished friend, and losing him as a result of my own self-centered actions.

I have learned from Yankee to pause and consider how blindly pursuing my own desires may impact others, especially those closest to me. But this practice of not doing harm isn't something I can accomplish once and for all. I will never dance through life in blameless bliss. None of us can. Life is too complex for that, and we have to take actions without knowing everything, especially when we are young. And despite our remorse, we can't fix the past.

While I can't go back and repair what I did to Yankee, I try to honor him and to make amends by pausing before I speak or act, to do my best to avoid harming others in my pursuit of my own desires. My efforts often fail, perhaps more often than not. But that feeling of blamelessness—that awakening from dread and terror to the tremendous, blissful relief that, at least today, I haven't harmed a beloved—that feels a lot like happiness.

2

PAL – RENUNCIATION

The surprising power of letting go

My stomach tight and twisting, I stood at Pal's door—as I often did. I needed to dig deep for courage to earn time with Pal; I had to knock on the door and ask the neighbor if I could take him out. I would pause on the dirt path before going up to the step to the door, a familiar, dreaded burn rising in my face and moving through by body. But my desire to be with Pal was so strong, it pushed me past my embarrassment. I liked to pretend that Pal, a strikingly handsome shiny black cocker spaniel, was mine, but he actually belonged to these next-door neighbors on Rockaway Lane. He was a friendly, calm dog whose pendulous, glossy ears and soulful eyes gave him a compelling earnestness, speaking of trust and friendship. I had lost my puppy Yankee, but Pal was still there for me.

This day, as always, after I brought myself to knock, my neighbor smiled down at me as I stood, hovering nervously on the concrete step.

"Have you come to take Pal out to play?"

I nodded, relief flooding me, and she ducked back into the kitchen, returning with Pal on a thin lead, his stub tail wagging madly with anticipation. We headed together towards the sliver of woods behind my house. A man parking his car nearby called out, "Handsome dog you've got there." I skipped a few steps in delight, Pal bouncing at my side. "Yes, this is Pal, my Pal!" I called out. We darted together into the woods and ran across the soft brown leaves to my favorite place, Eagle Rock.

On the rock, I could perch high among the quiet trees surrounding us, the warm light of the sun playing across the leaves and grass at my feet. Up there, I was closer to the trees and sky, drawn up into their glowing green and gold by the height of the rock. Sometimes I came to Eagle Rock with friends—playing cowboys, running with Patty and Freddy and Adrienne—and sometimes I came by myself. But the moments with Pal, like this one, were particularly special. There was nothing awkward, nothing missing.

Pal liked the fresh young grass at the base of the rock, and so did I. We sat in harmony, each of us sucking on the sweet stems of the newest growth, still soft and succulent. He lay next to me, and when I placed a hand on his thick and lustrous black coat, I felt the warmth of him pour into me.

But today we were not going to stay long at Eagle Rock. We had another destination. We left the woods and stopped in my yard to grab my red plastic bucket, then darted across the busy road facing my house to the gas station that hid the swamp behind it. We crept quietly around the back, unseen, into the stillness of the over-grown woods and the dark, cool water.

There was no one else there, just Pal and me in the swamp, our own secret world. I was free of pressure, free of any demands. We crouched under the low-hanging branches, slipping a little in the sticky mud, to get to the murky water's edge. There, with Pal at my side, I held my bucket ready as we waited and watched. I hoped today we might see or even catch a tadpole. Finally, after many attempts, when I swirled the bucket into the dark water and pulled it out, I saw a small sleek body thrashing back and forth. "We got one!" I told Pal.

I was entranced by the tadpole's muscular body and long tail and the tiny little legs just starting to grow. He thrust his tail rapidly back and forth, swimming round and round. I was gripped by the wish to keep the tadpole, to make him a pet. But he swam so desperately, he hit the sides of the bucket, and I could see he wanted to escape. When the sunlight started to fade, I slowly tipped the bucket, and together, Pal and I watched him swim free.

———

Not long after our tadpole adventure, I had to say good-bye to Pal. We took a final walk together, wandering aimlessly through the world we'd shared—the swamp, the woods and Eagle Rock, the swing set on the hill. But as the afternoon shifted to dusk, I knew I had to take him back home. I slowly approached the door of his house and bent down to put my head near his. I told him I was moving far away. I was sorry, but I wouldn't be able to take him to the swamp or the rock anymore. Then I stood and knocked and handed the leash to the kind neighbor. There was something so thick in my throat, I couldn't speak. She took Pal's leash and smiled. "I hope you like your new home," she said. As the door closed, I caught a final glimpse of Pal, wagging his short tail, happily at home in his kitchen. I stood for a time on the small concrete step, unable to move. The weight of sadness, the choking feeling, the pressure in my chest, it was like when I'd lost Yankee. But this time, as the pain came back clawing and gnawing, it came back with particular force—for I wasn't only losing Pal, I was losing my whole world.

The next afternoon, an enormous orange and white truck pulled up in front of my house. In a few hours, a team of men swept everything into boxes, carried it all down the stone steps, and then up the ramp and through the massive doors at the back end of the truck. I watched as the boxes with my ceramic boxer dog statues, my signed picture of movie star Chuck "The Rifleman" Connors, and my model horses—the palomino and the reddish brown one with the black tail held high—all disappeared through the truck's gaping doors. The doors clanged shut, the engine roared to life, and the truck pulled away from the curb. I stood frozen on the steps in front of our small white house, unable to look away, as the hulking truck rumbled off down the road.

Our house was empty, so we ate Kentucky Fried Chicken from a huge red and white bucket at the picnic table in our yard. Then all five of us, my parents and my brother and sister and I, climbed into the big green Chevy wagon. My father had one hand on the wheel, his other propped in the open window. My mother was bent over the map in her lap, peering at the yellow highlighting showing the best route to New Jersey. My sister and brother sat calmly, looking as if we were headed to some regular kind of event, like a swim at the local reservoir. But I craned my neck and twisted backwards, wrenched and contorted, as if my body were caught by the rusty garden hoe we'd left propped in the garage. In silent agony, I watched as my home and Pal's, right next to it, disappeared from view.

—

My family and I landed almost 300 miles away, in another world. Our new house, half of a two-family, was bigger and had a pond in the backyard. But I could hardly bring myself to explore it. It was something Pal would have done with me. Thinking of Pal, of my old friends, of my desk at school, left me curled up on my bed, a weight on my chest. I wanted to be able to go out, knock on a door, and have my Pal with me again. Even having my own room for the first time, even the new bedspread with the big blue and green daisies my mother had picked out for me didn't make me feel better. I had never minded being on my own before, but now I was floating, adrift, alone in a world I didn't recognize and one that didn't recognize or care about me. My whole body ached with the wish—the desperate need—to have my old life back, to run with my friends and with Pal, to feel again the sense of happy, easy belonging that I didn't even know I had until I found myself torn from it.

A few days after we'd arrived, as I lay on my new bed, I caught a glimpse through the window of the boy who lived in the other half of the duplex. He was about my age, and he had smiled and been friendly—even eager—when we met the day we moved in. Now he was rowing a small rubber dingy in the backyard pond. This was something I had never seen before or even imagined. I got off the bed for a closer look. The boy was floating in the boat, using the oars to dig down into the water and pull mud up. I went to the back door near my room and opened it just a crack, watching the boy as he examined the muck on the paddles. I took a couple of small steps onto the flagstone porch, keeping one hand on the door.

The boy called out to me. "Wanna get in?" He gestured to the other side of the boat.

I nodded and took a few more steps across the grass to the pond. The boy rowed to the edge, and I clambered awkwardly into the boat. It started rocking, so I grabbed the sides, crouching in the back, and the boat steadied. I could feel the cool surface of the water under the smooth rubber bottom of the boat as the boy rowed away from shore.

He took me on a tour, over to the tiny waterfall where a stream fed the pond and then to a gaping tunnel at the other end, where we could hear the rushing of water flowing away into the blackness. Then he let the boat float freely, oars up on the sides, held loosely in his hands. I sat staring, silent, clutching the sides of the yellow dinghy. He looked right at me, his brown eyes huge and intense behind his thick tortoiseshell glasses. "There are muskrats, leeches, and big bullfrogs!"

I scanned the pond to look for these mysterious creatures, the ripples of water circling out from us, calling us outward. This pond was like the swamp, my special retreat with Pal. I had lost him and the magic world we had shared, and the pressure in my chest was still there. But looking out at the pond, I felt my hands yield their grip on the boat a bit, resting a little more lightly on the wet, cool rubber. I thought of the tadpole Pal and I had found, swimming with his miniature tail right out of our bucket off into his big world. In this place, there were creatures I'd never seen or even heard of. And I could imagine—I could almost see—my Pal, still wagging his tiny tail in his

tidy kitchen. Pal would have loved this pond. But somewhere in me, I knew Pal was not pining for me. He was
happy with the life he found himself in, with or without
me, just as it was.

I saw in my mind's eye that Pal was okay. And here
right before me, the mysteries of this pond and its creatures beckoned, pulling me into a new world. I plunged
my hand down next to the boat, breaking the surface of
the cold, black water, and I looked up at my new neighbor. Drawing a big breath, I found the words: "Will you
show me the frogs and the muskrats?"

That day in the little rubber boat didn't change everything,
but it was a turning point. It planted the seed of a new
understanding: When holding on feels like the only thing
that will save you, it is the letting go of what you've lost,
of what you can't have, that takes you out of suffering,
out of the anguish of needing things to be different, and
into freedom and happiness. That day in the boat was the
beginning of a lifelong effort to resist the urge to hang on
to what I've had or wished for so I can be free of painful
longing and open to the joy of what is in front of me. To
let go, so that my hands and my heart are free to reach for
what is right here, right now.

Renunciation can be an off-putting word, seeming to
demand that we force ourselves to give something up, to

dramatically turn from what we most desire. That sounds harsh, difficult, and sad. But in Buddhist teachings, the Perfection of Renunciation is not about giving up. It's about the power of letting go—letting go of specific requirements for our happiness, of clinging to the need to have things a certain way, as I was clinging to my old life. In letting go comes freedom, freedom from the agony of wanting, freedom to find happiness in what is actually is around us.

With his eager, loving face and his full embrace of whatever arose, with his ability to adapt so readily to my arrival and my departure, Pal helped show me how it could be done. Pal was emblematic of all I'd had and all I wanted to hold onto from the happy, cozy world we shared. But Pal was also my guide in letting go of that world. He demonstrated the surprising power of renouncing what can't be so we can reach toward what *can* be. He showed me that by letting go of what we hold so tight, we can open our arms and embrace the glories of what is unfolding all around us.

3

TOOK – GENEROSITY

The ultimate act of loving others exactly as they are

My family arrived in New Jersey in the summer of '69, just days before Armstrong took his steps on the moon. One of our first nights in our new house, we gathered around the small black and white TV screen, watching those awkward, bold steps, the only sound a crackling voice sent to our barely furnished living room from outer space. Like the astronauts, we had landed on alien soil.

My new neighborhood was like an enchantment out of *The Chronicles of Narnia*. Across the street from our house, the massive stone buildings of a graduate school campus loomed at the top of a hill, monsters carved into their cornerstones. Men in long black robes strode along flagstone pathways, capes billowing and flapping behind them like the wings of enormous crows preparing for flight.

Beyond the paths lay a sweeping expanse of rolling green, broken by strange spots of white, which, when I drew close, I found to be abandoned golf balls. I turned one over in my palm, where it fit just right, hard and wet and smelling of the sweet cut grass that clung to it—a strange treasure.

Cresting the hill, a stone tower stood against the sky, enormous bells hanging at its peak. I could hear those massive bells even inside my bedroom, the bright, penetrating sound flowing down to our house at the base of the hill. The intricate, insistent melodies marked the turnings of the day, vibrating deep into my bones—a call to something, though to what, I did not know. At the end of our street a wide stone arch stood guard, an imposing portal to my new world.

Behind our house lay more mystery: a pond with deep holes along the shoreline, said to be made by elusive creatures called muskrats. If I stood quietly, I might see one— finally, a sleek head surfacing, cutting smoothly through the dark water before diving down and disappearing into the black depths. I stood entranced, my jaw agape, tasting the musky, pungent air on my tongue, as rich and thick as the soil where the muskrats dug their holes.

In this wondrous, foreboding new world, there was so much. But so much was gone.

There was no more TV tag or playing cowboys in the dirt with my neighborhood friends. And it wasn't just the games that had changed. At school, my new teacher Mr.

Goodheart took us out to the playing fields and had us lie with our heads on each other's stomachs. He called it Grokking. It was nothing at all like my school back in Massachusetts, sitting next to Mrs. Mulcahey's desk, reciting the four times tables and getting her nod of approval along with another gold star.

On the long walk home from my new school one day, as I passed a stately brick house, two girls giggling on the front steps pointed at me and called out "The two yellows don't go!" They turned to each other, laughing. I looked down at the bright gold culottes I was wearing and the white and yellow striped cotton knee socks, my favorite outfit. No one had ever laughed at me before, not like this. I put my head down and pushed my bike past them as fast as I could, their taunts burning, my face as hot as when I was roasting at the beach.

The boys in my class were equally sure I was a loser. They had decided, upon inspection, that my legs didn't have the right shape and that I was "fat." Desperate to fit in, I tried things that I never would have done back home in Massachusetts. I joined the kids who stole Mr. Goodheart's cigarettes and tested them out behind the bleachers.

The one thing that remained unchanged from Massachusetts was my yearning for a dog. In my old town, I'd lost one dog and borrowed another. I saw their faces when I shut my eyes, flooded with an empty, aching yearning. But my parents had been adamant: *No dog.* Our failed experiment with my puppy Yankee had left them reluctant to try again, and our lives were busy and complicated, especially as we all adjusted to our new world.

But then, not long after our move, my dad's line suddenly changed. Perhaps seeing that I was struggling, he wanted to help me adjust. Or perhaps it was not just *my* heart that had a hole in it. My dad, after all, had arrived to work on a campus under significant strain, including admitting women for the first time and handling demonstrations about the Vietnam war. He was also in a strange new world. Whatever the reason, one day he offered, "If we're going to get a dog, let's get a *real* dog. Certainly not a dachshund." And then, after a pause, as I held my breath, he said the words that would change my life—and his: "A beagle, for instance, now that's a real dog."

My dad had all but proposed we get a beagle. And I knew he was a man of his word. He absolutely never retreated from a promise. Suddenly, after years of pestering and begging and wishing and hoping and my shame-ridden failure with my puppy Yankee, there was an opening.

A couple of weeks later, I came home from school and watched my mother pull our big green Chevy wagon into the driveway and step out. In her arms was a small, wriggling beagle puppy. I ran to him, and my mother passed him to me. I held him, his solid body fitting into the curve of my chest as if he was meant to be there, filling that carved-out space in my gut.

People walking through the campus and the local park wanted to meet my adorable pup. I quickly got used to explaining his odd name, Took. The family who raised him from birth had given the puppies names from a line in a classic children's poem by AA Milne. But there were not quite enough names. There was one extra pup, so they named him for the next word in the poem, which was "took." He looked like a classic beagle, with a compact frame, friendly face, soft flopping brown ears, freckled legs, and a black and brown midsection. "He is three-quarters beagle and one-quarter Irish setter," I proudly told anyone who asked—and many who didn't.

Took's name was assigned with a certain randomness, but it came to reflect our close relationship: He gave generously, and I took. With Took as my constant companion after school, life in my new world changed. Every day when I got home, he looked up at me, ears out to the sides and slightly lifted, as if to ask, "What shall we do today?" He and I wandered the paths and hallways of the graduate school buildings up the hill, where all the doors were open, inviting endless exploration. With Took by my side, the fortress-like stone buildings seemed less dark mystery, more magic, and those castles on the hill and the pond behind our house became our secret play worlds.

Took and I roamed the basement corridors of the graduate school, shooting pool in a recreation room and exploring the dark stone passages. Behind our house, Took sat with me, trapping leeches from the pond and watching for muskrats. He waded with me through the culvert under our road, a secret tunnel from the pond to the golf course. There, Took and I would collect golf balls—he was the best finder—and wash them in the little boxes mounted on posts, set there just for making golf balls bright, bright white, like little glowing planets.

Every afternoon we went to a playground at a park nearby. I had often encouraged Took to accompany me on the slide, and one day after I climbed the narrow, steep metal steps to the top and whizzed down the shiny chute, Took trotted around to the ladder, and, just as if he'd done it his whole life, climbed to the top, one paw at a time. I stood next to the slide, cheering him on. A mother with two little kids paused to stare. I watched, jumping up and down in place, as Took stood briefly at the top of the slide, looked down, and then slid, standing, all the way to the end, and onto the dirt. We all clapped spontaneously, and I bounded over to Took, telling him what a brilliant boy he was. As I was hugging him, the mother told me she was impressed at how I'd trained my dog. I basked in her praise, and didn't say a word about Took doing it all on his own.

It was a trick that never got old. The attention and praise he drew made me feel I could belong in my new world. With Took as my buddy and confidant, regardless of what happened at school when I came home, I had an eager friend waiting for me, welcoming me, an antidote to navigating the perils of girls who teased and tormented me and boys who, instead of being playmates as they were in my old neighborhood, now rated and rejected me. Took's loyal, warm presence made everything just a bit more manageable.

———

Took had quickly become an integral part of my dad's life too. Together, they were a fixture on the university campus. It was in an era before leash laws, and we lived at one edge of the college. As I got ready for school each morning, Took would set off at a brisk trot with my dad, the two of them fast and purposeful walkers, heading to work—my dad, with his wiry build and his wavy salt-and-pepper hair, striding in his loafers and tweed jacket with the elbow patches, his tie flopping over his shoulder in the breeze, and Took at a trot, nose down, eager for the journey.

After accompanying my father to his office on the campus, Took would come back home on his own, about a half-mile trek. Sometimes, however, he would stay for a while before he made his way home, lying quietly under a table in my dad's office, providing a calming distraction for stressed students seeking grade changes and diplomas. I visited my father's office frequently. One day I came in the back door and found my dad moving rapidly up and down the row of tables in the long open space of the office, pacing back and forth under his iconic "zero errors" poster, printed by the massive mainframe computer that was automating all the grading systems for the first time. When he saw me, my father immediately stopped in his tracks and beamed. "Ellie!" It was his special name for me; no one else used it, and it warmed me every time.

Crushed by worries over how I was struggling in a class, I drew close to my dad, and we moved to a quieter area of the office to sit down together, near where Took was lying peacefully under a desk. I spilled out my story. I couldn't do the math. I was scared I'd fail.

"Are you thinking you might drop it?" he asked me. With one hand on Took and my eyes on my dad, suddenly the crisis seemed soluble—even simple.

———

Took became known on campus. "Hey, isn't that Took?" was a common refrain. A brief break with the beagle provided moments of relief and respite on a campus where cultural change and the pressure to achieve could make things tense. My dad, whose position entailed registering all the students and handling all their grades, was in the thick of it. But with Took by his side, the two of them drew smiles and made friends far and wide. As part of his role, my father was also a popular teacher of sports sociology and was warmly dubbed "Coach" by his students. The combination of his easygoing, enthusiastic teaching style and the cheerful energy he and Took shared made them approachable even during turbulent times. As they strode along together, Took's lips parted, his tongue hanging slightly out in a dog version of my dad's smile. Joy and ease flowed from them, expanding to include anyone who passed. The interactions were usually brief comments about Took's fascination with squirrels or the latest campus basketball or football scores while the passerby stroked Took's ears and petted his soft, strong back. Though quick, these simple moments of joyful engagement were like gossamer threads weaving the fabric of the community together.

My dad accepted everything about Took with great fondness—even his habit of barking persistently. One summer day as I leaned against the railing of our back porch, I watched as my dad stood, newspaper in one hand, looking down at his dog, whose front feet lifted slightly from the ground with every insistent, sharp bark. Other fathers might have yelled or shoved the dog. My dad did neither. He quietly, almost pensively, asked a question: "Why is he barking at me?" Took kept barking, and my dad asked the question again, still quietly, but this time directly to Took: "Why are you barking at me?" There was no judgement or frustration in his words, only curiosity, only a wish to understand his beloved dog. This communion of call and response ended only when Took seemed to tire of it, retreating to the shaded spot by my father's lawn chair. With Took settled, my dad sat down in the chair and turned to his sports page. Took sighed. Their duet was complete.

My father relished Took's escapades. One day he had to go find his beagle, who had been serenading a female dog at a house about a half mile away. The family had found our phone number on Took's collar and called, asking us to collect our dog. When my dad got home, he was grinning. "Took was out there in that Samoyed's yard with five other male dogs. He was the smallest by far." He cast an admiring look at his beagle. "He pretended not to know me at all!" my dad laughed. "He dug his paws into the ground and lowered himself so I just about had to carry him out of there," he said, shaking his head. He smiled down at Took, now happily curled up on his afghan. "Yup, he's a real *hound* dog," he said, a hint of his native Memphis creeping into his voice.

I'd seen a friend's father kick a puppy for getting underfoot when greeting him at the door. But my dad gently accepted Took just as he was, no matter what. No matter the inconvenience to him, Took was being Took, and for my dad, that was a glorious thing, something to celebrate. This deep well of generous spirit could be missed if you heard my father's strong opinions, which he didn't hesitate to share. The price of fish, the pace of municipal projects, or the progress of the Cleveland Browns, his favorite football team—all were targets for his skepticism, even scorn. But when it came to Took, he didn't offer opinions or judgements. My father appreciated Took exactly as he was, and he set Took free to be completely himself.

With that freedom, Took lived his life to the max, right up to the end. As he aged, his passion for rabbit hunting evolved into a spectator sport. He would watch the bunnies from his favorite patch of sun in the driveway, and instead of dashing off as he'd used to, he would follow the rabbits with his nose, nostrils twitching, eyes faded, but still alert. When the end finally came, it was crushing. I was living in Boston by that time, and my mother called me to say that Took had died in a kennel while she and my dad were away in Florida. He had died alone, and for all he knew, abandoned.

My father never spoke of it. The early loss of his own father and the realities of life in his generation had taught him to pick himself up and move on, not to wallow. But after Took died, it became apparent that he never really recovered from the loss. I avoided the tender topic of how Took died, but when I asked my dad about getting another dog, he said he didn't feel he could take on the heartbreak of losing another one. "I will miss Took until the day I die," he said. Coming from a man who spoke volubly on politics and sports but very rarely of his feelings, those few words telegraphed a sea of pain and were instantly seared into my memory.

Those words have haunted me. With my dad now gone, I know that the weight of loss in my own heart is permanent too. My father didn't use the word "love," a word as startling and inappropriate in our family as other four-letter words. But refracted through my memories of my dad with Took—his joy in Took's escapades and even in his annoyances—I can see more clearly how my father's unjudging love, even if unspoken, let me explore, grow, and thrive too.

Recalling my smiling father coming in the door with the wayward Took, my mind sweeps back through six decades to times when my dad was there for me as I stumbled along, trying to find my way. When I dropped out of math in high school, he told me, "This decision will close doors, not open them," but he left me to make my own choice and supported it. When as a young teen I wanted to travel to far off West Virginia to see my dear friend who had moved away, he drove me hours and hours to get me there. When I toured colleges with him and pondered one school versus another, including doubts about the beloved university he worked for, he declined to put his thumb on the scale. Even into my fifties, I looked to his unjudging understanding and belief in me. One day I called him to talk about a potential life change. My dad had become thinner and frailer, but when I asked him how he was, his words, as always, were light and chipper: "Doing pretty good for an old crock!" We laughed, and I told him I wanted to know what he thought about my leaving the suburb I'd lived in for decades to move to the mountains, seizing what seemed a last chance to pursue a persistent dream. He listened, paused, asked some questions, shared some thoughts about weighing risk. Then he offered words that have hung in my mind and heart: "But Ellie," he said, "only you can paint your own portrait."

As I made my way into my sixties, my own daughter grown, my father in his eighties, I wanted to drink in everything about him and his life. On weekly calls we talked about his childhood, the loss of his father, his friends, and what he most wanted to share with his grandchildren. In one conversation, I asked him for the first time about his approach raising his children. Did he have an intentional plan of some kind? He was clear. "Oh yes. I wanted to be careful not to build houses for you. I wanted to give you the materials to build your own houses."

Through the mirror of his joy and acceptance of Took, I see reflected this unspoken, open-hearted love of my dad's: letting me build my own house, paint my own portrait, even when inconvenient for him and even when he saw perils. In his twenty-fifth college reunion book, my dad wrote that his children "were fascinating when little, but they are even more interesting as they become, each in his own way, his own person." Just like with Took, who he never judged or tried to change, he truly saw us, he supported us as individuals, and he offered us the rarest love: the pure, simple desire that we emerge into our true selves, trusting that we would flourish in our freedom.

When I was afraid and unsure, my father—like Took—constructed a world of safety and love for me, not with words but with an unceasing flow of the most generous kind of love, love without strings, without reference to their own needs. Both of them, every day of their lives,

offered that rarest of invitations to me: to be utterly myself. A door thrown wide open for a full-on chase.

When contemplating being generous, we often think of
measurable things like possessions, money, and time, and
these have an important place in Buddhist teachings about
the Perfection of Generosity. But the teachings reach fur-
ther, to intangibles: to giving protection and giving love.
My father was very generous with his money and time,
but it is this kind of giving, this generosity of spirit, that
for me is the fullest expression of his life and legacy. It is
only now, seeing him through the clarifying light of his
relationship with Took, that I can grasp the power and
significance of what he shared so unstintingly with me—
unjudging, fully generous love. The way he loved Took,
with curiosity, appreciation, understanding, acceptance,
and with unvarnished delight. This is the lens through
which I can truly see my father's pure love for me.

My father's gift to me, to Took, to all those he knew
and loved, was an antidote to our world's exhausting and
divisive grading system, a system built from bricks of
judgement by an unending process of continually com-
paring and assessing, by defining things and people as
good and bad, right and wrong, and trying to control and
shape them accordingly. His relationship with Took half
a century ago still projects the limitless light of what he

offered: love that cherishes, without evaluation, obligation, qualification, or expectation. A love that transcends the spoken words "I love you," offering a springboard for a life of one's own choosing, one's own making, a life of freedom and happiness.

4

BUDDY – PATIENCE

Peace that comes through engaging with what is, not in grasping for an imagined ideal

It was still dark when Dr. Bell struggled through the back door of the veterinary clinic, a cardboard box in her straining arms. Even though it was early, the three vet techs—two other young women and I—were gathered in the exam room, prepping for the day of appointments and surgeries. Dr. Bell put the box down on the exam table, her head hung low over it. We paused, instruments and cleaning cloths suspended in our hands. The predawn dark of a late November day pressed, noiseless, against the windows of the small room. For several long breaths, no one moved.

"Not sure they're going to make it," Dr. Bell said, her voice muffled, her uncombed hair hanging in clumps, hiding her face.

"The puppies?" one of the techs asked, her voice quiet, tentative. Dr. Bell bred dachshunds, and the staff knew she had been anticipating a litter.

There was no answer, and no sound from the box.

Then Dr. Bell looked up a bit, her face pallid and puffy under the fluorescent lights, flesh hanging loose, as if her bones had given up holding onto her features. Her polyester tunic strained across her torso.

She began shuffling around the room, gathering a bag of fluids, a towel, a needle for an IV. The other technicians and I moved quickly to assist her, one of us grabbing a heating pad, but Dr. Bell brushed her aside, and we all pulled back, moving closer to the box. We peered in, and then, as each of us in turn looked up, we glanced among ourselves, faces grim. The most senior tech shook her head, the slightest of movements.

Dr. Bell came back to the box, and carefully drew one lifeless body up and onto a towel she'd placed on the cold steel of the examination table. The puppy's eyes were shut, and its egg-shaped form wasn't yet identifiable as a dachshund. The puppy lay, unmoving. As Dr. Bell began fumbling with the needle and IV bag, the senior technician approached, hesitating.

"Do you want some help?"

The words seemed to break the vet. She slumped over the puppy, picking the tiny form up and cradling it in her trembling, chapped hands. "Nothin' anyone can do. Not gonna make it. None of 'em."

A thread of sound, a stifled whimper, arose from the table, but it didn't come from the puppy, or from the box. It came from Dr. Bell.

We glanced quickly at each other, shifting our feet, all three of us taut with unspent action. The senior tech tipped her head slightly in the direction of the exit, and we silently followed her, single file, towards the door. I was the last one. As I passed the examining table, I glanced at Dr. Bell, still hanging over the limp shape of the puppy she'd placed on the towel. One of her hands was on the puppy, the other upon her chest.

———

That day was a turning point. Those moments with the dead puppies, and the heartache, marked the end of a dream for me. It wasn't because the puppies died—they were Dr. Bell's pets, and their death, while terribly sad, wasn't because they'd received inadequate care at the clinic where I worked. Still, those stark moments crystallized the disillusionment, sadness, fear, and confusion that had slowly engulfed me in the months I had been working at the veterinary practice. I'd been chasing a dream I'd nurtured since I was twelve. My family's vet, Dr. Clark, who was still caring for my dog, Took, generously took me on in the practice he shared with Dr. Bell. I was a twenty-one-year-old, fresh out of college, armed with a psychology degree, a love of dogs, and a vision of what it would mean to be a compassionate veterinarian.

It was a vision honed through repeated readings of James Herriott's books about being a country vet in Yorkshire, England. At first I helped out at the vet clinic as a volunteer, but after a few months, Dr. Clark started to pay me. I was taking courses at the local college to fill in gaps for vet school—math, organic chemistry—subjects I'd skirted before, sure I would fail. This felt like my last chance to realize my dream.

The very first day I began working at the clinic, I met Buddy, a liver-colored pointer sprinkled with freckles everywhere except for his rich auburn ears and several large spots on his back. He was a "donor dog," living at the clinic so that he could be available to provide blood should a sick dog need it. His health was attended to, but his life, between meals, was mostly waiting. The technicians tried to be kind, tossing him a treat or riffling his soft ears, taking him on short outings around the clinic grounds. But they were busy. Buddy didn't appear unhappy, resting quietly in his cage, and he responded with interest and even joy when the staff engaged him. But when I looked at him, his world so limited, I saw nothing but the huge gap between his current life and what I felt his life should be: Running free, like my beagle at home.

I asked Dr. Clark if I could take Buddy into the nearby woods. He said I could but warned that "It may not be good for him to have that kind of change." I was sure Buddy would love exploring the trails.

Our first outing was grand. Buddy seemed happy walking under the trees with me, even though he had to stay on a leash. We walked for a couple of miles, Buddy with his nose to the ground, sniffing, and then, suddenly, his head up, ears forward, alert. He was, it seemed to me, fully alive. When I brought Buddy back to his cage, I promised him I would take him out again soon.

The next day, I found Buddy scratching desperately in his cage. The lead vet tech explained that he wasn't used to the woods, and being out had stirred up allergies. I tried taking Buddy out again, and he pranced with delight, but the result was the same. He enjoyed his outing, but it was followed by hours of tormented itching.

I stopped taking him to the woods. He had been content with his lot before he met me, living the life that presented itself, enjoying what was available to him, not looking to what was not. I had fancied myself Buddy's savior, but all I had done was cause him suffering.

Buddy's life, though, was not the only way my dream of being a vet ran aground. Early on in my time at the clinic, Dr. Clark was blunt. "Female vets are a waste. They take up limited spots in veterinary school. Then after a year or two of practice, they quit to have babies."

He had hired Dr. Bell to help in his practice, but he didn't seem to make comments like this around her. She often seemed downcast when she arrived at work. One day, as I was cleaning up the exam room after a euthanasia, she spoke softly into the silence of the room: "This job will break your heart."

Heartbreak was mostly what I felt there. The surgeries I assisted with were not the heroic, life-saving miracles of my imagination. They mostly rendered cats and dogs unable to reproduce or altered them for human convenience.

"It's actually an amputation of the first joint of each toe," Dr. Clark informed me as I prepped a cat for declawing. I had to peer hard to look beyond my discomfort to the care and the healing.

I petted Buddy every morning and continued to set up and clean up the exam rooms. But I was distracted by what seemed like a terrible choice facing me. Instead of a becoming a passionate champion of animals as I'd dreamed, I now saw only two options: I could harden my heart, as Dr. Clark seemed to have done, so that none of the surgeries or compromises bothered me. Or I could give my heart over to the animals and break it in the process, as Dr. Bell seemed to have done. When my boyfriend came for a visit, it was a welcome diversion from this confusing tumult of emotion stirred up by caring for the animals and weighing, every day, if I had what it took to be a vet. It wasn't just organic chemistry in the way. It was my heart.

My boyfriend was in graduate school several states away, and we hadn't seen each other in months. He offered to treat me to dinner at a nice restaurant, something we normally could not afford. I was excited to see him and be together on an unusual outing. But as we entered the fancy dining room, I walked awkwardly in a dress and pointed shoes, so different from my usual jeans and sneakers. I felt phony trying to choose from a menu of dishes I wasn't familiar with, squirming in the soft seat. And then, there in the dining room, my boyfriend reached across the table, presenting a small jewelry box, a beautiful sapphire ring sparkling against deep blue velvet.

Was there a beat before I responded to his proposal? Not then. But I feel a beat now, my memory reshaped through knowledge I didn't have then, that my thirty-year marriage to this gentle and brilliant soul would end in shame and sadness. All I knew then was that a person I cared deeply for wanted to spend all his days with me— the often nervous and neurotic me.

His proposal was wonder and magic, and it also set a clear course for me through the sea of confusion that had engulfed me. With the ring and the plan to marry, there was an exit path from my torment at the clinic. I didn't have to see Buddy balled up quietly in his small enclosure, feeling as if I were somehow complicit in his constrained life. I didn't have to watch the tortured Dr. Bell spiral downward or see more cats and dogs in pain. I didn't have to prove to Dr. Clark that women could be great vets or push on with a futile effort to pass organic chemistry and get into vet school. The spell of my long-nurtured dream was broken; I saw only the yawning chasm between what

I had envisioned and what was real. A new road away from it all called to me.

My last day at the clinic, I spent a few extra minutes with Buddy, my whole chest aching, seized with unspent tears. I took him for a short walk on the brown grass outside the clinic. His mouth was softly open, his tail swaying lightly from side to side. We stopped near a tree, and under the chilling grey sky, I told him that he was the best boy. My throat was tight and my words sounded choked, but Buddy wagged his tail more quickly. I could hardly bear to look at him, and I turned to take him back to the building. As always, he went readily back into his cage and curled up, seemingly at peace.

A few hours later, I got into an aging white Dodge Dart donated by my grandmother, gripped the steering wheel and, eyes on the road to Boston, hit the accelerator, leaving the ever-patient Buddy and my dream in the rearview mirror.

For years, when I thought about Buddy, it was with anguish for a dog whose life was so limited, so far from what I pictured as ideal—just as being a vet turned out to be so far from what I'd imagined. All I saw at the time was flawed reality that I couldn't fix, not for Buddy, and not for me. What I didn't see was how, in patiently embracing the world that was actually around him, Buddy was content. He didn't compare his lot with that of other dogs but found contentment in the good things—meals and treats, the moments of attention, the short outings.

In Buddhist teachings, the Perfection of Patience, as Sylvia Boorstein explains in her book on the Paramitas, is about "abiding in the moment" and embracing the view that "peace is possible, right now, whatever the circumstances."[2] This is not a call to passively accept difficulties but, as Victor Dougherty has written, to abide with them, even "turn towards" them,[3] "accepting the truth of life's unsatisfactoriness," as a BBC guide to the Paramitas explains.[4]

I was not comfortable abiding. I was far from being able to accept, let alone embrace, the challenges and imperfections of a world I'd idealized. I fled from the face of the patient Buddy. I fled from the challenges, conflict, and confusion in the complex world of veterinary medicine. It's not that the decision to pursue a different career path was a mistake but that I lacked the patience to accept the reality around me and to take the time to make a calm, fully considered decision. I was too caught up in that gap between real and ideal.

When I left the clinic, I still saw Buddy as a martyr and myself as his failed savior. Over the years, I began to see something else. Buddy was not suffering. He was abiding with what was. And in doing so, he found peace. I still struggle with a restless urgency to pull away from anything that doesn't quickly align with my image of what it should be. But the image of Buddy's soft face and wagging tail will always be a prompt to pause, to abide, to embrace what is—not passively, but with active acceptance and patience.

5

GIZMO – TRUTHFULNESS

*Facing and sharing even the starkest
truth releases an enormous power*

The tiny puppy, with the color and lively bounce of a wolf in the wild, seemed almost unbearably sweet. He had come to us through a "broker," an intermediary who had promised to find us a Pomeranian puppy from a reputable breeder. He had just joined us in the small Boston apartment I shared with my new husband and was sniffing and darting around our battered couch. In a few short bounds, he disappeared into the bathroom. He emerged a few seconds later with something oblong and brown sticking out of his miniature mouth.

"He's got a cat poop!" I yelled.

My husband ran for the pup, grabbed him, and tried to extract the offending item from his mouth. A bear of a man, not given to dramatics, he suddenly released the puppy, and shaking his hand, shouted: "He bit me! He bit me!"

Blood flowed from his thumb. This was no nibble from a teething pup—the adorable little Pom-Pom had suddenly used his teeth as hard as he could, with significant results. Stunned, almost disbelieving, we scrambled to contain him in a small pen and focused on patching up my husband's wound.

We weren't sure at first what to call our puppy, but that first day delivered up his name: Gizmo. This little guy bore a striking resemblance—in looks and personality—to the character Gizmo in a popular movie of that year, the original 1984 *Gremlins*. The movie star Gizmo was a creature with big round eyes, pointy ears, and a fluffy face, eerily like our puppy. But the connection went deeper. The Hollywood Gizmo and our puppy shared a Jekyll-and-Hyde personality: friendly and docile unless exposed to particular conditions, then all too ready for violence. The darling and the devil.

At twenty-four, I was wildly happy to have my own dog for the first time, having lost my beloved childhood beagle just a few months before. With my husband immersed in graduate school and me still new to Boston, Gizmo and I established our own routine, heading to the Esplanade along the Charles River every morning and every night. I learned how to groom his double coat, and I tried to read up on training methods—the biting was a serious problem. I would open the books at night, but after a few pages, I would toss them down. It seemed to be all about proving you were the boss. I didn't want to be anyone's boss. I wanted Gizmo, like my childhood beagle, to be my friend.

One spring afternoon, the sun bright and the river sparkling, Gizmo and I wandered on the Esplanade, which was full of people relishing the return of the sun. A couple approached, hand in hand, strolling. "Oh! How sweet!" the woman called out. I braced myself. She would want to meet him—the adorable Gizmo. She bent down to pet him, crowing, "He is *so* cute! What kind of dog is he?"

I stood, smiling stiffly. "He's a Pomeranian." My mind was spinning, assessing risk. He'd never bitten a stranger—only me, and a couple of times, my husband. I told myself he would not bite this woman. I was sure. Well, *pretty* sure. Finally, the people moved on, and I drew air back into my lungs.

I felt compelled to pretend I had this adorable friendly puppy to hide the truth that my cute pup was a ticking time-bomb. I didn't like constantly faking, constantly being on edge. I went back to the books. The recommended methods were the "alpha roll" and using a choke collar—sometimes violently—for control. The experts called these methods asserting "dominance," the best way to train a dog, they said. Something in me recoiled, but while highly practiced in following instructions, I had no experience in questioning authority. I tried not to see that these training methods were based on inflicting fear and pain.

One early morning, walking out on the wide path next to the river, Gizmo lunged for a bone left behind after a picnic. Afraid to be bitten, I grabbed the leash tight, the recommended choke collar squeezing his throat. I had to get him to release the dangerous bone. I pulled up on the collar and shouted "Drop. Drop. DROP!" Gizmo snarled and clamped down harder on the bone. I was afraid of being bitten, and I did what the professional trainer in the book said to do. I swung him on the leash. The way to show you were the alpha, the boss. Gizmo held the bone tight in his teeth, growling, snarling. I clung to the leash with one arm and tried to grab the bone with the other. He lunged and snapped. I jerked back, my heart quivering and darting in my chest like a cornered gerbil. I was aware of people passing and staring, and I felt the heat of their stares, burning. The need to hide, to hide who my puppy really was—who I really was—tore at me.

But there was no place to hide. Every few weeks, out in that public park, Gizmo would grab a piece of trash, then stiffen, snarl, and clamp his jaw. Some days I collapsed and let him eat his treasure. Other days, I kept up the fight. Whatever I did, the result was always the same, and it wasn't what the books promised. Gizmo got the precious bone or burger bit, and we walked on, my head bowed, blind to the beauty of the river beside me. Our outings were a careful dance around pain and fear.

There was a painful dance in my marriage too. My husband was mostly absent, off at all hours at the university where he was deeply enmeshed in graduate school. Much of the time I was alone—or that's how it felt to me. I tried not to say anything when he came home in the wee hours, but words are not the only way to cast judgement. My tension and sadness were, no doubt, obvious enough. The space between us grew.

My failing efforts to connect with my husband left me feeling alone, and worse, unlovable. One winter night I stood alone in the shadowed confines of our apartment, staring out at the lights glowing in the windows across the narrow street. Right in view, dozens of people were living happy, normal lives while I stood in the dark, abandoned. Who would want to know—let alone like—someone unable to manage a cute puppy or a new marriage, whose closest relationships were a lie? I crept into bed, pulled the covers over my head, and wept into the darkness.

A day or so later, I was on a lunch break, wandering in the upscale mall that surrounded the office where I worked. I drifted aimlessly along the faux brick walkways, passing J.Jill, Ann Taylor, and Abercrombie, staring blankly at the perfect but lifeless manikins in the store windows. I could not take my eyes off them. I was a poser and an empty fake too.

But the next morning, out on the Esplanade along the river, Gizmo pranced next to me, his red coat shining, and as we turned a slight curve on the path near a footbridge, a huge flock of Canada geese came into view, grazing on the grass. Gizmo took off, barking wildly in his glee, running full speed towards the geese. Just as he came close enough to nip their feathers, they rose up in synchronized flight. He didn't catch a single goose, but he carried himself differently that day, head high, curled tail aloft. Watching him, a witness to his unbounded joy, my own spirits soared with his. That evening, instead of staring out at others' happiness, I sat reading on the worn couch, one hand on Gizmo, curled beside me. Perhaps we could be the pals I'd wished for, living in peace and joy together. Leaning back, stroking him, I let myself believe he was a normal dog—and that I was a normal person.

——

That state of suspended belief worked well to sustain me, even across years of ups and downs. I pretended the problems had resolved, and I told myself that Gizmo's good days outnumbered the bad. But the struggles and the conflict persisted—not only with Gizmo, but in my marriage: My husband and I had reached a crisis point after a wrenching move to another state.

We were living in an aging apartment in upstate New York that we'd rented only three months before. He had left his graduate program, and I had started one. By extracting us from our Boston life and bringing my husband here, I'd added to the vulnerability in our marriage. The change, I had imagined, could be an opportunity for a reset for each of us and for our relationship, and my husband had generously agreed to come. But nothing was going as I'd hoped. Just outside the windows of the new apartment, trucks roared by in a relentless torrent, surging in the blackness. I felt the traffic's ceaseless pounding as a deep pulse in my chest, a drumbeat proclaiming my failure: I'd made a huge mistake in coming to this graduate program. Just the day before, I'd forced myself to pretend, yet again. To smile and nod in a conversation with classmates, as if it made sense to me that Pee Wee Herman was a serious object of study.

And now, here we stood in our living room; the pressure of the hammering noise was merciless. If I didn't flee, I would explode. My words tumbled out, unfiltered: "I'm going back to Massachusetts, and I'm taking Gizmo. Whether you come or not." My soul, laid bare by my desperation, did not shimmer prettily. In crisis, I would save myself.

"*Whether you come or not.*" The words hung, suspended. Then the tsunami of sound from the road engulfed us.

Though my words were harsh, as a practical matter, the choice was clear. We were only in New York for my graduate program, so within two weeks we were on the road back to Boston, together. I made sure I had everything I needed, right there in the car: the keys to the new apartment, and Gizmo. Despite our challenges, he had become my buddy, my anchor. My husband, driving the U-Haul truck, had our cat and our few possessions—a jumble of cheap, unattractive furniture we'd found through want ads.

———

We landed back in Massachusetts on tenuous ground, battered by having parachuted out of graduate programs. We were scrambling to find our footing professionally and as a couple. But my daily walks with Gizmo connected me to the new suburban neighborhood. Every morning, Gizmo and I would greet a friendly, buoyant couple who brought their Shelties to play in the field across from our house. Gizmo—who was typically indifferent or aggressive with other dogs—seemed to enjoy being among them. He and I would watch as the Shelties flew after Frisbees, their long shiny coats rippling in the light of a new day. Out there each morning, life seemed simple, joyous. We found our rhythm. And when I would return home from work, Gizmo was unfailingly there to greet me, wagging and rubbing against me, his face a consolation and relief as I tumbled into my thirties.

Gizmo softened a little as he matured. He had even become a beloved participant in family gatherings. My father—a cheerful, accepting man—particularly connected with the quirky little guy. At Christmas holidays, he and Gizmo and I would gather each evening at the fireplace, seated together next to the warm flames. Everyone else was settled in their beds, and Gizmo and my dad and I would sit at ease in the dark, my father's cigar glowing, his glass of whiskey close at hand, long iron tongs for tending his cherished fire at his side. It was precious time, time to ask the real questions, time to be in my father's calm, full presence, to absorb his clear view of the world, a healing balm. I'd ask about a problem I was having at work or to hear more about his childhood in Memphis, drinking in his words. Gizmo's silent presence, lying next to the glowing embers, seemed to open my dad up as much as the quiet dark, as much as the whiskey. "How's my grand-dog?" he'd ask, leaning to scratch Gizmo behind the ears. It was a term of endearment he used for the dog even after actual grandchildren began arriving—including my daughter.

My husband and I had become parents, arriving home from Russia with our adopted daughter when Gizmo was eleven. By that time, Gizmo was to all appearances a staid, harmless, elderly dog. But despite this age and his mellowing, I knew I could not fully trust him, certainly not with a vulnerable child. I set up gates and made sure he and my daughter were never in the same room at the same time. The arrangement left me perpetually vigilant and anxious. I felt worried for my daughter but also bad for Gizmo, who was getting less of me than he was used to.

One day during my daughter's nap, I leaned over to touch Gizmo as he slept curled on the couch, hoping to give him some extra attention. He lunged upward, tearing at my face. I recoiled in shock, my hand to my mouth, fingers slippery with warm blood.

I ran to the bathroom and looked in the mirror. My upper lip was sliced open from just below my nose, down through the lip itself. I didn't feel any pain, but I could see that the Band-Aids I had in the cupboard weren't going to fix this. With my husband at work and no access to a car, I pressed a cloth across my mouth and got my daughter from her crib. "Here we go! On a special trip!" I told her, trying to sound cheerful as I put her in her carrying sack and headed for the bus, and then the subway, to the urgent care clinic.

The physician peered closely at my face and the long, deep wound. He stood back. "To align the top of your lip properly is delicate. We could get a plastic surgeon in here to do the stitching so it lines up right. But you'd have to wait."

I looked down at my daughter, crawling on the floor in the exam room and thought of how soon she would need to eat, how long we'd been in transit, and all that was ahead of us to get home.

"Please, just sew me up," I said.

——

The truth stared back at me every morning when I looked in the mirror, the ragged stitches replaced over time by a white scar. Like me, my daughter could be permanently disfigured. She could be deeply harmed by this dog.

The problem was clear, but the solution was not. Even with all the challenges his biting presented, Gizmo had accompanied me, grounded me as I painfully sought a path in life. He and I had shared walks every day and a bed every night. We had been close companions for more than a decade. And there were considerations related to how my daughter came to us. I needed to protect her, certainly. But beyond that, what would it mean if we gave away the dog she cooed and crawled for, because he was flawed? What message might that send about what family meant, what adoption meant, what love meant? And the darkest questions of all: Hadn't I fueled the cruel cycle of Gizmo's aggression? Was I so different from Gizmo—afraid, ready to bite, if necessary, to protect myself? If he was a monster to be cast aside, I was too.

Though I had kept Gizmo's secrets along the way, I wasn't willing to endanger others by lying to rescue groups about his history of biting. As I called around and put out flyers, the response was always the same: "I'm so sorry, but we don't accept dogs who have bitten." I had to admit to myself that the prospects for a new loving home were nil. Even aside from the enormous barrier of his biting, Gizmo had developed epilepsy and an adrenal condition that had left him with sparse fur and a bare tail, all conditions that were likely the legacy of irresponsible puppy mill breeding. No one was willing to take him in.

Then one day, while I was sitting next to my daughter in the back yard with Gizmo nearby, he twisted abruptly and grazed her cheek. I pushed him aside, grabbed my daughter, and ran into the house, picturing the blood flowing from my own face not that long ago. I sat her in her highchair in the kitchen and examined her carefully, finding barely a trace of contact, just a pinprick. I sagged with relief. But the reality was inescapable. I had not protected my child—what kind of mother was I?

Desperate, I went to see my trusted, long-time veterinarian, a fatherly man. He tipped his head as he listened to me. With his wise, soft eyes upon me, I let the words spill out, finally. For the first time, I revealed the full truth about how serious the problem with Gizmo was, about the long history of bites, about what had happened to me, and now the very close call with my daughter. I paused. "I don't know what to do." I slumped over Gizmo at the exam table, spent, emptied by the effort and the relief of having come out of hiding.

It was the vet who broke the silence.

"He's a small dog. I think a dental specialist could grind down his canine teeth."

He explained that with flattened canines, even if Gizmo were to bite, the bite wouldn't pierce skin. He thought it could work for a small dog like the twenty-pound Gizmo.

I looked up at the vet, scanning his gentle face to be sure I'd heard this right.

I pushed out one shaky word: "When?"

And so the specialist ground down Gizmo's two sharp teeth—teeth used only for biting and tearing, not for eating or for anything else. Gizmo became, for the first time in eleven years, safe to be around. After the procedure, perhaps because Gizmo grasped that he didn't have the bite power he'd once had, he stopped protecting objects or lunging to bite.

A state of truce, or perhaps, something a little bit like trust, emerged. A new path forward, forged in the clear light of truth.

—

When Gizmo was just short of his eighteenth birthday, I went to the kitchen one morning and found him immobile in front of the refrigerator. He lay there, inert, his skin blackened and exposed under his sparse, dry coat. I drew a sharp breath, falling to the floor to kneel next to him, my hand stroking his head.

That day in the kitchen, I didn't see the struggles Gizmo and I had had. I saw only the companion who'd been with me on a long, wild ride—a journey of nearly twenty years, through the trials and challenges of graduate school, motherhood, and the loneliness and sadness of a difficult marriage, where connection never took hold for long. I gathered Gizmo into my arms and rushed to the vet. At the clinic, they swept him into a back room and emerged quickly to tell me he was in advanced kidney failure. He was dying.

I said goodbye to Gizmo as he lay unconscious on the sterile, cold surface of the examination table, my hands resting on his side, my eyes blurred. All the pain, all the fear, all the hiding, was soldered into those final moments. But so was love—a certain kind of love. The kind that grows like a seed struggling under insufficient light and without quite enough water, but with just enough to press itself out of the soil, feeble and bowed, but alive.

———

The soil, water, and light in my marriage had been insufficient for both of us, for years. But we soldiered on. We were committed. We were parents who wanted stability for our daughter. We cared for each other. We'd been together since we were nineteen and did not know adult life without each other. Yet the pain was always there, as was the sense of treading delicately at the edge of an abyss. Surely, though, I could fix this—hadn't everyone said marriage was work? And then no one would ever need to find out that I was an unlovable person.

I thought about ways we could mark a fresh start. New wedding rings seemed just the thing. And this time, they'd match. I found two silver rings, lightly carved. I hid the box and nervously awaited our twentieth anniversary.

When the day came, I brought the wrapped box to my husband, seated at his usual place in the dining room, and extended it to him. He undid the bow, opened the box, and glanced briefly inside. He didn't look up. I knew in that moment, before he said a word, that my idea was a disaster.

Though he was kind and gentle about not wanting the ring, it was a decade and a divorce before the pain of it became less blinding, before I could see what I didn't see then. My gesture with the rings was not just inept, it was self-centered. It was I who had always wanted matching rings, I who cared that my husband didn't wear a band. It was I who concocted an inane plan to cover the chasm that had grown between us with a superficial symbol of unity—not a way to heal, just another way to hide.

He carried his pain. I carried mine. The harm we'd caused each other was unintentional, but the wounds were no less deep and no less real than if we'd gone at each other with savagery in mind. What no one had said when they professed the need to work at marriage: some wounds fester. They don't heal.

———

For many months after his death, Gizmo's ashes sat on a shelf in a handsome wooden box. It was a constant reminder of our complicated life together—a life of companionship and of struggle. Catching sight of the box brought a twisted feeling in my gut.

One spring day, I impulsively grabbed it from the shelf and marched out into the back yard. I took a shovel and dug a deep hole in the far back corner of the garden, under the forsythia bush that grew thick, its branches curving heavily over a hidden, dark place. I shoved the box of Gizmo's ashes into the hole and covered it with soil.

———

The ashes lay buried for thirteen years as my daughter grew and left for college, and new, less challenging dogs came to share my life. But the ashes were not the only thing I'd buried. I'd done my hiding very, very well: No one expected it, but my thirty-year marriage was finally ending. I made the long trip to see my father to tell him I was getting divorced.

He'd been married to my mother for almost sixty years, and divorce—or a violation of any commitment—was essentially unheard of in our family. I was very worried about how he would receive my news. But as we stood in his kitchen that lovely June morning, the sun streaming in, my father's response was characteristically concise, clear, and honest. "That's so sad," he said, sagging a bit as he stood at the counter.

He and I stood closer than usual, leaning in.

"Was it at least good at the beginning?" he asked.

I looked up tentatively into his dear face and his blue, blue eyes, a little faded, but still so bright against the pure white of his hair. I saw the pain there, his pain for me, and my own eyes welled.

I drew a deep breath and released it. The air flowed out from my lungs, and with it, the weight of hiding, the desperate effort of thirty years to make sure that no one would see, no one would know how I'd failed. How I had failed in my marriage, just as I had failed with Gizmo.

I pulled myself up and let my eyes rest fully in my father's. I felt his gaze holding mine, soft, sad, but not judging, only accepting. I had revealed my darkest secret. And yet he was still there, standing with me, together in the warmth of the sun streaming in from the window.

———

When my father died a few years later, it was sudden and quick. I yearned to draw him back to me in any way I could and offered to clear out his things. There wasn't much. My dad was exceedingly frugal and cared less about possessions than anyone I've ever met. In his last months, he'd spent most of his time seated in his favorite spot on his old, ragged couch, one shoe sporting a silver duct tape repair, a hole in the knee of his favorite jeans. There was room in his budget for new shoes and new jeans, but not in his life philosophy.

A man like that doesn't leave a lot of stuff, and what he leaves, it signifies. I started in his bedroom. There was not much in his bureau, but as I pulled out what was in the narrow top drawer beneath a few carefully matched and balled pairs of athletic socks, I found two pictures he'd held onto. Just two. One of them was of Gizmo as a young dog, after his wolfish coat had turned red and before it thinned. His face was bright, his eyes eager, fixed on something beyond the camera. I stared at the dog in the photo and sucked in a breath. He looked—happy.

My father didn't keep pictures around. He had hundreds of slides in the closet, but with rare exceptions, they were only of his favorite subjects: birds and landscapes. Yet somehow through the decades, in his sparsely filled sock drawer, he'd held onto this particular picture. He'd kept it even knowing the origin of the slim white scar on my upper lip. Even knowing Gizmo with all his flaws, my dad had held onto—and, it seemed, treasured—this picture and the memory of Gizmo, his "granddog."

I collapsed onto the edge of his bed, clutching the image, unable to look away. I could see, I could feel my father. I saw him as he was the day I had told him my thirty-year marriage was ending. That day, I had basked in the redemptive power of truth: being accepted exactly as one is, without hiding, with flaws and failures laid bare. And now as I sat on his bed, my father was with me again, presenting the same profound gift. The anguish and corrosive shame of keeping secret my cruelty and failure with Gizmo was washed away by my father's choice to hold Gizmo—with all his imperfections—so close, for so long. The picture in his drawer was an absolution—for Gizmo, for me.

In Buddhist teachings, the Perfection of Truthfulness includes not only speaking truthfully, but the requirement to start by being honest with ourselves, to break through the compelling desire to protect our own egos or reputations, to let go of the desperate wish to maintain the appearance of being good and having it all together. Yet when being truthful will require facing one's own failings and facing blame and shame, it is tempting to hide behind falsity. The falsity might not be lying. It might be simply avoiding speaking the truth, a withholding that seems to offer a refuge, a place to save ourselves. But what I learned from trying to cover over problems with Gizmo—just as in my marriage—is that deceiving others, or ourselves, about our true circumstances doesn't save us. It isolates us. Instead of helping us avoid shame, hiding the truth feeds shame, the shame of carrying secrets, the shame of pretense. It took multiple decades and a damaged dog for me to recognize that facing and sharing even the starkest truth releases an enormous power: a power that can draw us out of the darkness and shed light on the path to happiness.

6
WILLIE – ENERGY
Expressing and directing our life force

After the disaster of my graduate program in New York state, my husband and I started to rebuild our lives in the suburban town outside Boston where we'd rented one half of a duplex. Gizmo and I developed a new routine quickly. Every morning as the sun rose, we crossed the street to wander through a small wood.

On one of my first walks, as I emerged from the trees onto the nearby athletic fields, I caught sight of two women with two Shetland sheepdogs, playing Frisbee. Gizmo didn't like most other dogs, so I usually avoided them when we were out walking. But as I paused where the trail met the field, I noticed that Gizmo was standing quietly on the grass, his body loose, with no sign of stress. I felt my shoulders relax as we continued to move slowly along the edge of the field, making our way closer to the Shelties.

The two dogs were focused on their Frisbees. With the unwavering, keyed-up attention characteristic of herding dogs, one of them fixed her eyes on the plastic disk her person was holding up and crouched, front paws shifting back and forth, every muscle poised for action. Then the woman, with a sudden snap of her arm, threw the Frisbee, and the Sheltie was off in a blur of honey and white. With a great leap, she caught the Frisbee mid-air, then dashed directly back to the feet of her person, dropped the disc and waited, tensed, for the next throw. The second Sheltie was not far off, sniffing the grass. When the other woman called, he ran to catch another Frisbee and brought it back too. The game continued like a highly choreographed dance routine, with Frisbees whirling and dogs flying into the air, then swirling back to their people in circle after circle of joyous athleticism.

As we walked closer, the Shelties didn't seem to notice Gizmo, and he remained interested but at ease. Perhaps it was their undivided focus on Frisbee-chasing that made Gizmo comfortable with them, but in their presence it seemed that he was awakened and captivated by their energy. So was I.

The two dogs were stunningly beautiful with their long, rippling coats, uplifted ears, and keen, penetrating eyes that were locked onto their people. The dogs were immediately responsive to even the most casual gesture from hand or arm, rapidly anticipating where the Frisbee would go next. They acted with a speed, excitement, connection, and eagerness that I'd seen only at dog shows. We walked around the field until we were very close to the Shelties. I drew near, waved, and called out, "Beautiful!"

Unlike their fired-up and laser-focused dogs, the Sheltie people could have been mistaken for yoga teachers. At six or seven in the morning, even though they were getting ready to go to work and managing two active dogs, they were calm, smiling, and unrushed. Wired a bit like a Sheltie myself, I was typically walking fast, scanning the environment for dogs Gizmo might have issues with. But the Sheltie people would smile and pause to greet me when I saw them out on the field in the first light of day. Their smiles were genuine, inviting connection. Meeting up with them and watching their dogs at play started my day with peace and pleasure.

Gizmo still had issues—he had bitten me a few times and was living with the challenges of epilepsy and an adrenal condition. And I was working two jobs, trying to find a solid career path. But our time out on the fields each morning was a respite from all the problems. The dogs were so in sync that the Sheltie people and I started to call Gizmo an "honorary Sheltie." Watching those talented athletes brought joy and a sense of freedom. Freedom from vigilance, from the demands of work, and from the worries weighing on me as I rebuilt my life.

———

One day, after relishing these shared mornings together for about a year, I was standing next to Gizmo, talking with the Sheltie people about their latest litter. They were breeding thoughtfully and on a very small scale, devoting more and more time to showing their dogs. As we spoke, one of the women looked up at me and asked whether I might be interested in one of their puppies. I was stunned—*one of these amazing, responsive, brilliant, gorgeous creatures? One of their precious puppies? Mine?*—but my response came quickly: "Yes!" Being trusted with one of their puppies, these dogs who were the center and focus of their lives, was humbling, exciting, and a huge responsibility.

I told them there was one snag. Our landlord would not permit a second dog. "We are thinking of buying a house, though, and the puppy could join us as soon as we move."

The two women looked at each other and then to me. "I think we could make that work," one of them said. I was grateful and delighted and on fire to find a house.

A couple of miles from the apartment in the same densely populated town, we found a home that seemed perfect. There was a small yard, a playground across the street, and a slip of woods nearby. It seemed just right for Gizmo and workable for our Sheltie too. As soon as we were settled, I arranged with the Sheltie people to have their six-month old puppy, Willie, join us. They had decided he would not stay in their breeding and showing program, and so he was available.

Willie was a classically handsome tricolor Sheltie, mostly black with tan markings above his eyes and on his legs, and white on his legs and across his gorgeous, full ruff. He had a thin muzzle and bright attentive eyes and could direct his perky ears almost like antennae. He was quick, smart, and fast. I could hardly believe I was living with such a spectacular creature. I was a mere mortal; he was magical.

It quickly became apparent, though, that now that we were living together in close quarters, Gizmo was un- settled by Willie's Sheltie energy. So many things stirred Willie into a frenzy, and I understood Gizmo's skeptical, cautious look when the puppy was in one of his frequent whirlwinds. My tight schedule made managing him chal- lenging. On workdays, after getting both dogs out for walks and getting though my own routines, I typically had about three minutes to dry my hair and then run down the hill to catch the only bus that would get me to the office on time.

One morning I was standing in the bathroom, glanc- ing nervously at my watch as I turned on the hair dryer. Willie, who'd been watching from the hall, started barking fast and sharp, darting up and down, pouncing towards the offending object and then pivoting away again. As the dryer roared, his barks became more insistent and in- tense. He catapulted himself into the living room, kitchen, and back to the bathroom. His tension was at a fever pitch, and it felt as if it pulsed not just in him, but in me. I had to escape. I pulled the plug of the dryer, grabbed my bag, and ran out the door, leaving Gizmo staring out the window and Willie flying from room to room.

Willie repeated this frenzy every time the dryer was on, no matter how much I tried to get him used to the sound. He could hear the dryer from anywhere in the house or the yard. His intensity and the high-pitched fusillade of barks were like electric shocks, whipping me up into a panic.

In those first weeks together I tried to carry out regular routines, like cleaning the house, but Willie would dart and nip, herding the vacuum cleaner. When I turned it on, he responded as with the hair dryer, darting, dashing, barking, working so hard to get that offending machine under control, that I ended up like a wild thing myself, strung as taut as a tightrope. When we got into these charged whirlwinds, I lost the ability to manage Willie patiently and effectively. I couldn't think at all. It was like my brain short-circuited under the intense energy radiating from Willie.

Raking leaves brought out Willie's avid desire to work too. One day I tried to rake up the oak leaves and had him out in the yard with me, thinking it would be a companionable time together. But Willie couldn't leave the rake alone. I put him in the house, but he dashed from window to window, his paws scratching on the sills. With only half the yard raked, exhausted and worried about what was happening inside, I gave up.

I knew Shelties were active and needed to have plenty of exercise, and I tried to quell Willie's drive by finding outlets for all his keen, eager, engaged energy. There was a bike path down the street, and on a sunny fall day, I decided to see how we would do as biking partners. I mounted my maroon five-speed and took off, aiming to match the pace of Willie's brisk trot. We flowed along, Willie shifting briefly to a lope and back to the steady, strong trot. We were moving smoothly together, and the joint action felt like being truly in rhythm with him for the first time. Yet I knew the arrangement was perilous. If he were to stop suddenly or jump in front of my bike, we could both be seriously injured. I watched carefully and counted on Willie's intelligence, industry, and focused understanding of the job at hand. As I pedaled, I felt the fresh air on my face, and with Willie in perfect synchrony at my side, a sense of peace and rightness suffused me. We were so connected, it was as if we were one being.

When we got home, Willie was more peaceful than I'd ever seen him. He even rested for an hour or two. But that outlet for his energy didn't change his fundamental drive: to announce and address every noise and movement at home. Later the same afternoon, he was herding house-hold objects and the mailman yet again. Calling him to me after he surged to the window, barking, I sighed. The biking had been marvelous, a hint of what was possible with this remarkable, super smart, driven dog. But there were limits to how often I could get him out on such long rides. Gizmo needed slower, shorter walks, I was working full time, and there was the rest of life to take care of.

I went biking with Willie a few more times and tried to get both dogs out for frequent walks. But given all the constraints, nothing seemed to settle him for long. I found myself, like Willie, on edge, perpetually vigilant. I couldn't avoid what was right in front of me: He was restless and frustrated. I wasn't giving him the life he wanted and needed, a life where he could be happy. There was no respite from the sense of failure. My joy faded along with Willie's.

"Willie just can't settle," I told my husband. "He knocked Gizmo down—he is just so energetic, and Gizmo seems intimidated. I'm afraid Gizmo will be seriously hurt one of these times."

My husband had sensed the heightened level of vigilant energy in the house. Neither of us saw a simple solution. "They trusted me with him. They waited for us. How can I go back to them and say something's not right?"

There was no easy answer to that question. But as we spoke, it became clear that since Willie was still a puppy, this would be the best time for him to find another home. I had not wanted to admit to myself that perhaps his best future was not with us. Just letting that thought in made me want to collapse with the shame of failing this brilliant, stunning dog who'd been entrusted to me.

My enchantment with the Shelties and the honor of the breeder's offer had led me to jump in, thinking I was fully prepared to give Willie the right kind of home. I had fallen in love with the Shelties as they soared and leapt and moved with such grace and intense intelligence. But I didn't foresee what daily life would be like, especially given Gizmo's very different needs. I didn't have any inkling of how much less Gizmo would seem like an honorary Sheltie when he was actually living with one.

The call to the Sheltie people was one of the hardest of my life. "I am so incredibly sorry–I just can't seem to give Willie what he needs. And it's not working out for Gizmo." I felt heat pulsing in my face and a sickening churning in my gut. But once the words were out, relief washed through me. And the breeders—who'd never once been anything but kind, empathetic, and calm—understood.

"Shelties aren't for everyone," they said. They would be able to find him another home and even had one in mind.

The day I returned Willie to their house, I could hardly meet their eyes. He ran back into his old home, rushing from room to room, tail wagging, eyes alight. I hadn't earned a wrenching goodbye, and I left quickly, ducking into my car and speeding away, nauseous with shame. As I drove, the familiar but dreaded monsters in my brain pounded out their judgement: *Selfish. Phony. Unworthy.*

Willie went to live with a family on a large property in a distant suburb, where he had more to do, more space, and a higher energy home to match his internal rhythm. I tried to tell myself he was not harmed by my releasing him, that he actually benefitted. But to fail such a supremely marvelous being was a blow to everything I thought I knew about myself. His name fittingly captured the very core of his spirit. He had a tremendous will for life, an unlimited capacity for spirited and focused engagement. He gave his all, always, with the full force of will and energy: to connect, to protect, to partner. In that sense, Willie was perfect creature, a perfect creature I had failed.

It is tempting to shape my memories about Willie in a way that lets me off the hook. I could deflect the responsibility from me to Gizmo; certainly Gizmo's needs made things more complicated. But ultimately this was on me. What I see now is that it was a mismatch of life energies. Herding dog experts point to these dogs' tendency towards hyperactivity and restlessness, to being anxious and stressed, and to excessive activity indoors. And the founder and leader of an assistance dog training organization has written that even the most dedicated and astute dog trainers and dog lovers can have mismatches with dogs—relationships where their energy together, despite their strengths as individuals, creates dissonance. I see now that was the case for me and Willie.

In a way, the problem was that we were too alike in our nervous energy. Living with him was like living with a canine version of myself—high strung, easily overstimulated, insistent upon urgently carrying out whatever was deemed work. I was deeply drawn to Willie's energy, but our common intensity sent us spinning apart rather than uniting us in a shared rhythm. Living with Willie revealed something that should have been obvious to me but that I hadn't consciously recognized: I craved ways to calm my anxious energy. Situations that stirred my energy up left me feeling fragmented, my brain fried.

I think back to Willie's gorgeous shining black coat, set off by his white feet and cinnamon eyebrows perched above those intent and intelligent eyes. I can see him tearing across the grass, barking—smooth and strong. His mind, heart, and body sharp, crisp, and alive, every move conveying his infinite willingness to learn, respond, and work as a team. With the right kind of training and commitment, with better understanding of my own nervous energy, I should have been able to manage—even relish—life with this magnificent creature.

Willie's flashing eyes and dashing form, his pure vital energy for life, his vibrant spirit, his bracing engagement of every moment at full speed—all of this is so sparkling clear in my mind's eye, a vivid reminder of the beauty and the power of his abundant life force, which drew me to him. But my memory of Willie is also sobering. With Willie, I learned that bringing together an admiring human and a marvelous, willing dog, even if they love each other, is not enough. Living closely with a dog involves balancing energy, drive, and excitation in ways that yield comfort and joy for everyone. When it works, you don't even notice the delicate dance of energy. But when it doesn't, you can feel it in your gut.

This kind of mismatch is perhaps not so different from what can happen in human relationships, as I was to learn in my marriage. That was also a partnership that began in love and with great intentions, but where ultimately, we didn't find balance or shared rhythms. Yet, with the healing distance of time, it's sometimes possible for me to see that in my marriage, and with Willie, releasing one another was a profoundly sad thing but also a good thing. There is solace in freeing those we love to better lives.

In Buddhist teachings, the Perfection of Energy looks to the life force flowing from us continuously and how we use and direct it. An essential basis for that practice is noticing what our energy feels like and how it changes in response to what is around us and inside us. My struggles with Willie reflected that our internal physiologies, our deeply embedded, fundamental approaches to using our life energies, ultimately clashed. Like a singer whose sustained note of a certain resonance breaks a glass, Willie and I cracked rather than cohered. I learned from him how easy it is to misunderstand one's own capacity and needs, and in that misunderstanding, how one can harm those we love. And I learned from Willie how perilously difficult it can be to try to help others toward happiness.

I try to take some comfort in thinking that Willie found a world where he was free to express his own life force fully and that I've been able to apply what he taught me, as a parent and partner—and in all aspects of life—by doing my best to help others identify and find full expressions of their unique life energy too.

7

JASPER – WISDOM

*Acting with a wisdom that alters
how the world responds to us*

When my then-husband and young daughter and I opened the door of the small plastic dog crate and saw a bright little face peering back at us, there was nothing but wild excitement and joy. I was prepared to see a trembling, exhausted—and possibly sick—puppy. After all, this Pomeranian pup was only eight weeks old and had flown across much of the country by himself, separated from his mother and his littermates for the first time.

The little grey and black puppy, a miniature wolf whose expected red coat was not yet starting to show, pranced right out through the wire mesh door and looked up keenly at all three of us. Everything about his carriage said, "Cool. What's next?" It was close to my daughter's seventh birthday, and the pup had arrived in celebration.

He looked around with intense interest and then began bounding around the sunroom, exploring his new world.

We called his breeder. "He looks like he came from just across the street!" I told her. We sat on the floor, enchanted, as he explored the rug, the corners, the plants, and each of us. We were star-struck by this puppy who was so bold but so tiny that he could fit into our clasped hands. We called him Jasper, after the round red stone we knew he would come to resemble, though we almost immediately started referring to him as Jazz. The nickname suited his verve and natural ease in the world.

On one of our first outings, just steps out of the driveway, Jasper pulled on his leash with his tiny might towards a poodle puppy who was almost exactly his size. He wagged and sniffed and bounced a bit, clearly thrilled with this new pal. The poodle's people and I exchanged key facts about our pups—age, gender, origin, personality. The puppies didn't need these resumes; they were already darting around on the sidewalk in shared delight. Jazz had already found a fast friend in this curly-coated ginger snap of a puppy, Nellie. And as was to be so often the case, he planted the seeds of friendship for me, too, with Nellie's two moms.

"Let's meet up again to let them play," one of them offered.

Just a few days later, my daughter and I brought Jazz to play with Nellie at the playground across the street from our house. We discovered that the puppies particularly loved the sandbox. When Jazz sensed sand under his mini paws, he was inspired to wild speed. With sand flying, he barked and darted, his hindquarters tucked deep under him with each gallop as he propelled himself through the sand in mad bliss. Nellie supervised, dashing back and forth from the sidelines. Jazz broke into his sand frenzy to tussle with her again. Nellie's people laughed, I beamed, and my daughter cheered with delight. "My JJ!" she called out. She was so enchanted with her puppy, she had already given him a nickname.

The pure joy generated by these two bitty beings at play flowed in the spring air like a current, drawing puppies and people from houses that we'd never seen anyone come in or out of before. A snippet of a Yorkie pulled his six-foot person, a gentle soul as lean and wiry as his dog, into the park to join the fun. "He's never been interested in other dogs!" the man told us, his eyes alight, smiling.

Over the next few weeks, others joined the fun. Two standard poodles began to show up regularly for our playtime. They were adolescents from the same litter, a bit more composed than the small pups but still with the youthful keenness to meet other dogs.

A medium-sized black and silver poodle mix was drawn into the circle next, quickly positioning himself as the affable gentleman of the group, his person a master of wry humor. Then came an aging cream-colored standard poodle, who was happy to oversee the crowd from the sidelines while her people stood near, the man glowing with obvious pride and affection for his dog, cracking jokes the rest of us wouldn't have braved—but which made us all laugh.

All of these people had day jobs, but somehow we managed to get ourselves and our dogs to this swath of grass around six every evening. We'd arrive trotting at the end of straining leashes, faces taut with the exasperations of the day—the commute, the boss, the challenging relative, the dire headline—but after a few moments of watching the puppies cavorting in the grass or flying through the sand, the weight of the day drifted off into the gathering night. We began to know things about each other that were oddly intimate. The bowel habits of our furry pals. The inside scoop on who might be up for promotion. Worries about our children. In the warm circle of that playful, unjudging, and unfettered energy, the real stuff would tumble out and lose any negative force, carried off by the wild romp.

When the winter holidays came, we held a photo shoot with the dogs dressed for the event. We descended upon a garden shop, taking over their Christmas display, wrestling our excited dogs into position in a gazebo glittering with lights and ornaments. The standard poodles were doing their best to appear poised and dignified in their toy antlers; Nellie was sporting a special green scarf, her feet dancing and barking her "I'm in charge" bark; Jazz and another poodle jangled with every step, bells around their necks and feet. As the antlers began to slide off the poodles' heads, the bells chimed, Nellie yipped, and the dogs twisted, we tried to position them so they would all be in the frame, all looking at the camera, at once.

As we left, making our way across the parking lot in the dark, one of the poodles' people was laughing. "That was ridiculous!" she said. "But it was also one of the best Christmas holiday events ever, right?"

In the midst of our quiet neighborhood, Jasper, with help from his Nellie, had catalyzed a festival of poodles and puppies. He had a special kind of magic: an ability to generate good will. Just nine pounds full grown, he was not one of the small dogs that bark fiercely, in fear and defense, at any nearby dog. In Jazz's worldview, all dogs were friends. He approached dogs and people as if born to the knowledge that what he did would affect how others responded to him. One time he walked right up to, and then under, an Irish wolfhound—far more than ten times his weight and size—and craned his neck as high as he could in an attempt to sniff her most interesting parts. His assurance and his cheery confidence charmed her, just as he charmed everyone.

With Jazz, life was a party.

———

My daughter Nat was besotted with this teeny, strutting red ball of confidence. School could be confusing and tough, but her JJ never let her down. She came home from school dejected one day and sat slumped in an armchair in the sunroom. But JJ jumped up into her lap and sat there, alert. She snuggled him and reached for a book that was on the coffee table. She held it out to him. "It's called *Stories You Can Read to Your Dog,*" she said. "Are you ready?" He gazed at her, eyes alight, attentive but at ease. My daughter's voice took on the smooth rhythm of the story, and she stroked his thick fur and relaxed back into the chair, Jasper across her legs. She read on, holding the book so he could see the pictures.

Seeing my daughter so happy with Jasper, and knowing how she enjoyed conversing with adults, I wondered whether she would like to attend a therapy dog workshop with Jazz and me. It was 2002, and I had just heard about therapy dogs. With the cover of my sweet, talkative daughter and the adorable, self-assured Jazz, I felt perhaps I could try this out. I'd learned by watching Jasper: He entered any group with a bright, cheerful attitude and the bold assumption that he would be admired. The result was that he drew people and dogs to him, generating the mood he projected. I thought his style might lift people's spirits.

"We could take Jasper to hospitals and nursing homes and make people feel better. What do you think?"

"Sure!" My daughter was eight and up for most anything that involved Jasper or people. Both Jazz and Nat had a lot of social muscle to flex. It would be something special she and I could do together, and I thought of it as a kind of pay-it-forward plan. I figured that if I ever found myself in a nursing home, I'd sure want dogs to visit me.

I was a nervous wreck the first week of the therapy dog workshop, imagining the many ways things could go wrong. Jazz might act up; my daughter might hate it; I might have entirely the wrong personality for this. We walked into a community room at a local police station where the workshop was being held, and I quickly scanned the room. The instructor, in jeans and with thick reddish-blond, close-cropped hair, was smiling, standing easily at the front of the room while also clearly taking in each dog as they arrived and settled. She approached us as we entered and greeted us, with special attention for Nat.

"This must be Jasper! And his junior handler! So glad you are here!"

Nat was excited to meet the other dogs: a greyhound who had come with the second instructor; a large black standard poodle accompanying a friendly young woman in a wheelchair; a small curly white dog tended by a blond woman, who was grinning broadly; and a young couple glowing with excitement about their "baby," a sweet and muscular yellow Labrador. During the introductions, Nat told the group all about Jazz. She sat with the leash softly in her hand, chatting comfortably about how he liked to be carried in a special sack with his head poking out, how he loved tearing about in the sand, and how he chased snowplows. I leaned forward in my chair, feeling my shoulders relax just a bit. With Nat and Jazz as stars in the show, perhaps this just might work. Though I was nervous and uncertain right up until the last moment, in the end, we made it, all of us. Jazz had passed. We were on our way.

———

Our first stop was the local nursing home. I went to the facility on my own for an initial introduction as a new volunteer, with the expectation that if all went well, I'd return with Nat and Jazz for visits. As I spoke with the nursing home's volunteer coordinator and toured the facility and strolled the long halls, a long-buried memory flooded me.

Suddenly I was fifteen again, standing at the back of a hospital room, awkward in a white polyester dress with thin red stripes, the outfit required of volunteers. I hovered near the wall, far away from the bed where an elderly woman lay, her spotted and puffy hands listless atop the white sheets, her eyes upon me. I was sure she could see what an uncaring and stupid clod I was, that I was a complete fake as a "candy striper." My face pulsing, I twisted my fingers together, shifting from foot to foot. Her eyes still on me, I muttered "Um, I gotta go." And I slipped out of the room.

It was an experience I hadn't thought of in decades. But when the memory came, it came with force, and I again felt some of that old urge to flee. But I'd set Nat and me on this path, and I couldn't drop out now and disappoint her. I managed to refocus and get through the tour.

My daughter and Jasper and I forged ahead, arriving for our first official visit with Jasper's face poking from the carrying sack attached to my chest, designed for small dogs. We hovered at the entrance to the first room, and my thoughts floated briefly back to the candy-striper disaster.

"Would you like to meet Jasper, the therapy dog?" I called from the doorway.

The resident roused himself and turned his attention from the television. "Well, sure!"

As we advanced into the room, he caught sight of my blond-haired daughter, with her big pink glasses and light-up sneakers. He smiled, asking, "Who've ya got there?"

Nat launched in right away. "He's a Pomeranian, and he's only nine pounds! Wanna pet him?"

The resident stiffly moved one arm to reach Jasper's head. Seeing Jasper looking right back at him engaged him right away.

"How do you get him into that little pouch?" he asked.

"We just pop him right in. He loves it!"

Nat answered all the questions asked: What treats Jasper liked, when his birthday was, whether he was her pet. Sometimes her stories were more than any of the residents could follow, but they gazed at her and at Jasper, smiling.

Over time, we developed some particular friends. One was a man, Sam, much younger than most residents, perhaps in his early fifties. Unlike most of the others we visited, he was always out of bed, in his wheelchair. One day as my daughter and Jazz and I entered his room and approached Sam, his face lit up. "You're back!" he shouted, pulling himself towards us by using his heels to draw himself forward across the floor. He reached to pet Jasper's head and then told my daughter a version of the same story we heard from him every month:

"He's a good one you have here! Reminds me of my old dog. A poodle. Lively, like this guy!"

Jasper squinted his eyes with contentment, Nat smiled with pride, and Sam showed us the crackers he had, holding them out and asking if Jasper wanted any. These were small and simple rituals, and we didn't stay long. Yet Jasper's happy face seemed to brighten Sam's, as if a channel for joy had opened. When we left, I felt lighter.

The struggling patients, my daughter, and I—even the ashamed teenaged candy-striper version of myself that was lurking in my psyche—all of us were warmed in the light of the benevolent, ever-assured Jazz, who always took on the world assuming the best.

———

Jasper and Nat and I visited the nursing home for several years, and though Nat dropped out when middle school activities began to absorb her, her JJ continued to be among her best pals. Jasper continued to entertain and charm, both on his therapy dog visits and in the dog park group he had inspired. As the years went on, he accepted the arrival of first one dog and then, after her death, another. He hardly missed a beat, his spritely spirit undiminished, taking things in stride, as always.

As he edged towards fourteen, however, he started to slow down. I had taken to walking every morning in a local park, a rare spot where the now-elderly Jazz and my young golden retriever, Gracie, could both enjoy an outing. Gracie would bound through the park and look for her two besties, a male goldendoodle just her size and a pointer exactly her age and style—polite, fun, and friendly. These two lit up her world. While Gracie played and rolled and flirted, I carried Jasper up the steep hill and then put him down on the flat part of the path to walk at his own meandering pace. Gracie would be several hundred yards ahead and Jazz the same distance behind, so we were stretched out along the trail but were still a little band, together.

These morning outings were a lifeline for me, as the rest of my life was in upheaval. My husband and I had decided to divorce after thirty years of marriage, and we were in the awkward phase of living together while he was moving out. The anguish was compounded when I had a brief breast cancer scare, and then my daughter revealed that she didn't actually have the credits to graduate from college on schedule after all.

One afternoon, after my husband had moved, and no one but Jazz and Gracie and I were home, I went down into the newly cleared basement, my husband's things gone, and sat cross-legged on the floor, trying to take it all in. As I sat in the cool quiet, the reality of my new life—alone at fifty-five for the first time ever—washed over me. A howl emerged unbidden from my gut, a primitive, guttural wail that I didn't recognize as coming from myself at all.

My steady state, to the extent I found it, was with the dogs in the park in the morning. Being one of the regulars, chatting with the other dog walkers there every day, made me feel I was not alone, that I was managing, finding my feet in my new life. But then, on a lovely fall day, the temperature soared to ninety, unusual for the end of September. Jasper was out in the yard, and I needed to leave for work, so I went out to get him. He was seated on the grass, and when I bent down to talk to him and pick him up, he seemed oddly inert, and I saw that his tongue was a strange purplish color, and he was gasping for air.

My hands trembling, fingers fumbling, I managed to text the veterinarian, and he called me immediately.

The moment I mentioned Jasper's tongue, the vet cut in. "Bring him down right away. Don't stop to do anything. Just come."

I clasped Jasper to me, carrying him to the car. My jaw and entire body trembling, struggling to speak, I tried to reassure him, repeating "You'll be fine, buddy, you'll be fine!" over and over as I sped the quarter mile down the hill to the vet's office. The staff immediately took Jazz into the treatment area at the back. I waited. And waited. When the vet came out to see me, his face was set.

"We have him on oxygen. It's life-threatening. You need to get him to an emergency room. You need to go now."

There was a pause.

"You should know, he may not make it there."

My dear boy was dying. He had been happily enjoying our favorite park just the day before, but today, he was dying.

The vet and the technicians prepared Jazz for the trip to the ER as quickly as they could. They placed him in the back seat, his breathing slightly better from the oxygen they'd given him. He seemed calm, and his head was up, but he was still almost immobile.

"We're almost there, buddy. We're almost there. Hang on Jazzy, please hang on." My breaths were as labored as his.

As we pulled into the parking lot, I grabbed the nearest spot and turned quickly to Jazz. "We made it, we made it, you're going to be okay!" I told him. The staff in the emergency room had been alerted that we were on the way, and they swept him into treatment.

I was at work later in the morning when I got the report: Jasper had stabilized. I went to see him that evening. Expecting to see a very sick dog, instead I found him lying alert on a pillow in a cage, looking like his normal self, alert, bright-eyed, breathing normally. In charge of his world, as always. I cried as they opened the door and let me take him out and cuddle with him briefly.

But things were not what they seemed. The staff told me that they were not able to wean him off the oxygen; his heart was failing. They mentioned some tests they could run and treatments they could try. My brain folded in on itself with the effort of taking in this dire information while looking at my dear boy, seemingly restored to his full charismatic presence.

I left in tears, but with a thin strand of hope.

The next morning, my own vet called as I was arriving at work.

"I've spoken with the emergency team," he told me. "Jasper can't breathe on his own. He isn't coming back from this."

Then he said it: "It's time to let him go."

I walked up and down the sidewalk, turning over the vet's words. I had to let my boy go.

I arranged with the emergency hospital to be there for the euthanasia. I called my husband, who had moved out about six weeks before. Although it was a challenging way to reconnect, he had spent almost fifteen years living with this little dog, and I needed to ask if he wanted to be there to say goodbye.

We met in the intensive care area at the emergency hospital and sat side by side on the floor next to Jasper's oxygen cage. They put him in my lap. Tucked there, he didn't seem sick at all. He looked perfect—my charming power-puff of a dog, who'd never sent anything but vitality and light out into the universe. It was almost impossible to grasp that he would soon begin to suffocate without the infusion of oxygen.

We sat with him, and I told him how much I loved him. I looked down, curled over him as I cradled him in my lap, and my gaze rested on his exquisitely tiny eyelashes, those little rays of golden red, still glowing above his glistening, wise eyes. My Jasper was not afraid. He'd never been afraid.

I nodded slightly, and the technicians slid the injection into my boy. His head drifted slowly down. I bent over his warm small body, a stifled wail— like that one in the basement— wrenching itself from my chest.

The next day I was back in the park, a grieving mess, but Gracie needed her outing, and I did too. Since we didn't have Jasper with us any longer, Gracie and I were running together, our first journey there without Jazz.

That day, a trim, athletic man with a striking face— strong and knowing, but also gentle—passed us, running. I'd seen him many times in our early morning outings, doing multiple loops on the trails, even on ice, even in the dark. But today was different. He stopped in the trail a few paces ahead of me and glanced back.

"Where's your little dog?" he asked.

I tried to speak over the tightness in my throat.

"I lost him last night." I paused, lifting my head just a little to shift my gaze towards the man's kind, deep voice. "He's gone."

The runner turned his face fully to mine and reached to put his arm lightly around my shoulder. We walked together under the towering white pines, discarded brown needles soft and yielding.

"It is so sad when they leave us." His voice was low and rumbling, unrushed. "I always noticed your little dog. He never thought about stepping out of my way to let me pass. As if he just owned the trail," he said.

I felt a slight tremor at his words. He'd seen, he'd known, my little prince, Jasper. As we walked on, the topic of Jasper's death seemed to open up space for personal subjects. I learned he'd had losses too—a divorce, like mine, after decades of marriage. I felt as if this stranger saw me and knew me too.

Once home, the encounter held me. As if I were in a trance, I sat at the keyboard, words pouring from me. Words of thanks, of admiration for this person I didn't even know, for his kind understanding, for taking the time to care, for showing me, when I was so low, the very best in humanity. I had no plan for the words, I simply needed to release them.

But by the next day in the park, I had a kind of plan. I stood nervously on the path, my hand on a small folded piece of paper in my pocket—a page carrying all those words, to this man I now knew was Jaime. I saw him approach, running smoothly, as always. He stopped, as if to check in, and I hesitated for a second. Almost too quietly to hear, I said "I have something for you," and I quickly slipped him the small square of paper. He took it, glanced down at it, and then, looking up to me again, tipped his head just a fraction, smiled, and ran on.

I went to work, tormented by what I'd done. It was overreaching, over emotional, over bold. Over everything. I had no idea how my gesture might come across, but I was pretty sure it would seem strange and inappropriate. He would think I was crazy. I sat slumped on the floor in my office, my mind racing.

Into the depth of tormented replays of every stupid gesture I'd made, every overdone word I'd written, a beep from my phone penetrated. There was a text from Jaime. A short, sweet note with a simple question: Did I want to take a walk or run with him sometime?

The next morning in the park as I came running down the hill, Gracie in the lead, I saw him ahead. He stood in the playground under a huge, stately cedar. As he saw me, he held his arms out slightly, hands reaching towards me, palms up. I raced down the hill and stepped into his circle of welcome. Our eyes and hands joined.

This warmhearted, wise, and kind man was Jasper's final gift to me. I am not sure how to be grateful enough to Jazz, whose friendly confidence and interest in others was a key to happiness not only for himself but for me, for my daughter, and for so many others in our neighborhood and in the local nursing home.

Watching Jasper and traveling in his wake for so many years, I came to recognize and appreciate a special form of wisdom that he naturally and instinctively embodied. In Buddhist teachings, the Perfection of Wisdom focuses on seeing reality as it is, including acknowledging that things are always changing and are mostly out of our control. Jasper, a diminutive being, in control of almost nothing in his world, nevertheless generated connection and happiness everywhere he went. It took me years to grasp how he accomplished this alchemy. His special wisdom was to head into every situation friendly, confident, and inquisitive about whatever emerged. Those he interacted with, whether dogs or humans, reflected the same back to him. Jasper's approach was for me a revelation, especially since I tended to face the world with tension and anxiety. He built connections not only for himself but for me, making life seem like a simple circle: You open your joyful self to the reality of what's in front of you, assuming the best, and others, almost like magic, respond in kind. Jazz set up a reciprocity of goodwill and joy. We indeed control so little, but the wee wizard Jazz showed me that we influence so much, simply by having the courage and wisdom to step forward into the world with friendly joy and curiosity about what we find.

8

ISABEL – LOVINGKINDNESS

*The transformative power of
kind, unconditional love*

One of the three puppies was a ruby-red vixen, a dervish darting about the breeder's small kitchen. There were two black and tan pups, one shy, the other seeming to have come to life directly from the pages of the dog encyclopedia where we'd read that Cavalier King Charles spaniels were "sweet, gentle, playful, willing to please, affectionate, and quiet." My young daughter and my then-husband and I were smitten. We chose the adorable and unassuming black and tan, traveling home with her lying quietly on my lap in the front seat. My daughter, hearing that the breed had its origin in the castles of Europe, called out from the back that "she should have a queen kind of name, like Isabel"— and we all knew the moment we heard it that Isabel was her name. It suited this beautiful, composed, sweet, and soulful dog perfectly.

That night she slept against my chest under the covers, her gentle heart beating softly against mine. From that moment, I knew. Love was her only language.

———

With her gentle loving nature, Isabel was well suited for therapy-dog visits, and she was approved when she was about a year old. We began visiting the nursing home, as Jasper had. At every door, I asked "Would you like to meet Isabel?" Not a single person ever declined. Residents were immediately drawn to her wavy feathered coat and tail and to her calm, undemanding gaze. She looked like she'd been born into a litter of Muppets, with her big round eyes, impossibly long floppy ears, and fluffy cinnamon fur covering her feet like big fuzzy slippers. Isabel would sit or lie next to residents or, when asked, put her paws up on the edge of a bed so they could see her and touch her. Her gentle nature was like the peace of an opal sky on a November day, shimmering silver, asking nothing, simply offering quiet acceptance.

In Isabel's sweet presence, hearts swung open. On our therapy-dog visits, one elderly man told us about his own beloved dog every time we saw him. One afternoon, gazing fondly at Isabel and stroking her ears, he told us, "She is just like my old cocker spaniel, Jock." And then he launched into his favorite story. "Jock used to ride the commuter train by himself and get off at the right stop. Can you believe it?" He laughed and laughed, repeating

the story in loops, as if he and Isabel and I were on repeated runs of a brief, joyous rollercoaster ride.

Isabel's presence was therapy for me, too, on these visits. If I had walked into one of the patient's rooms alone,
just as in my teenaged candy-striper days, I would have
been nearly paralyzed with embarrassment. I tended to
feel awkward at social gatherings, watching myself trying
to play the expected role, wincing afterwards as I replayed
conversations where, yet again, I'd been dull or a fool or
both. Isabel changed all that. On our visits to the nursing home, she created a bridge to others that was wide
enough for me too. We'd enter a room, and the resident
lying in bed or seated in a wheelchair would beam. With
Isabel in the lead, my role was suddenly, joyfully easy.

Isabel and I were invited to visit with an elementary
school student who was terrified of dogs. She could not
cross the street to play in the park with her friends for
fear of a dog appearing, and her mother hoped a therapy dog might help her overcome this phobia. On our
first visit, the young girl, her thick auburn hair hanging
below her shoulders, green eyes fixed on Isabel, stood in
the doorway to her house, stiff with terror. Isabel moved
slowly and quietly, her eyes—always so moist it seemed
they might well over—offering an invitation to complete
trust. By the end of that visit, the child was holding Isabel's leash, helping to walk her. The next time we arrived,
as soon as the child saw Isabel coming down the driveway, she came a little bit towards her. By the time we left

that day, the child had laid her hand on Isabel's back. The third time she met Isabel, the young girl bent towards her and greeted her as a friend: "Isabel! You are here!" At the end of our few weeks together, the girl sat next to Isabel on the porch stairs, slowing stroking the dog's long ears. Bending over her rounded, smooth head, the child spoke quietly to her. "I think I'll be able to play at the park now," she said.

———

When I came home from work, Isabel would be resting near the door in her favorite chair, the one with the green leaves on the slipcover and the wide wooden armrest where she could watch out the window. Many days, I would find her with a single sock lying by her side. My heart melted as I saw her familiar face, her cheek against that single sock. It was always one sock, never more. Always one of mine. Tenderly, she had brought that sock to her favorite spot, not a thread out of place or a mark on it.

As I came in from work one evening and saw her with a sock, the strains and tension of my day fell away. I sat next to her and ran my fingers down her long wavy ears, burying my face in her warmth, breathing in the nutty-sweet smell of her as she wiggled and wagged with pleasure. After our ritual, I took the sock back to the wicker laundry hamper—where it stood, as always, undisturbed, lid closed. The hamper towered over Isabel; she was only about ten inches at the shoulder, a little over twenty pounds. I marveled at how she could have opened the lid, reached in and down, and extracted this one sock without tipping the hamper or leaving any evidence of her presence. I will never know how she did it.

But one thing I do know: With each and every sock, she spoke her love so well.

———

Isabel and I lived as tight partners through the years, and as she came into her full adulthood, we were facing a new challenge together, one she had inspired. We were going to attempt to run fifteen miles together. We were heading out for this bold challenge because about a year before, I had noticed that she had been putting on a little extra padding as she matured, and I had the idea that running might be good for her. Though I'd been a regular runner for decades, at that time, I'd had a persistent foot injury and hadn't had the courage to run in over a year. I was afraid the debilitating problem would return, but with the aim of helping Isabel—and with her companionship—I had risked running again.

Our first trial run was in the early morning, just the two of us, moving in harmony side by side in the pre-dawn light, the houses quiet and huddled close, slipping out before the pressures of work and motherhood and a difficult marriage closed in. We reached the peak of the long hill, and I looked toward the sun rising over the rolling green of the golf course and the smooth surface of the lake beyond. Isabel trotted next to me, her ears swaying, her mouth slightly open, tongue tasting the air. The pain in my marriage, the relentless pressure of work, and worries about my daughter's challenges at school were forgotten. A special peace filled me.

I got greedy for that peace. Running with Isabel felt so good, so right, that over time these morning runs together made me want to reach for more. I found myself, a middle-aged jogger, training for the Boston marathon. It was beyond anything I'd done before or even imagined doing. The training plan required long weekly runs, building up to a twenty-miler. So here I was, in late winter, facing one of the final long runs before the race: fifteen miles. The prospect made me jittery, and the night before, tossing and turning with worries, I had an idea. It would help so much to take this on with my running buddy by my side—my adaptable and companionable Isabel.

So there we were, at the door, together facing the fifteen miles. The distance was unfathomable. Isabel and I might have been heading out from our house in Massachusetts for New York, given how insurmountable the miles seemed. But as we gathered for our departure, the rest of the house quiet, the sun's glow just emerging at the edge of the sky, I was light with the energy of our new shared adventure, and Isabel seemed to be too. The start of our route was downhill, and we flowed down the middle of the empty street with a sense of utter freedom.

Given her size, Isabel was an improbable running partner, but we'd been training on short runs together for a while, and as we finished the hill and rounded a lake a couple of miles in, she trotted smoothly. I'd mapped a route that I hoped would distract us from the miles. It took us from the streets to a large conservation area, along trails there, and back to streets. The scents along the trail kept Isabel interested, and when we entered the woods, our heads were still high, legs fluid.

And so there we were, ten miles into the fifteen-miler, a mom pushing fifty who'd never been an athlete, loose polyester pants flapping, sporting a huge, heavy cotton sweatshirt, with a twenty-pound dog trotting by her side. We did not look like marathon material. We were running along a pond among towering pines, the softness of the trees and water easing our way. But I was beginning to tire, each leg lift harder than the last. As we left the trails and hit the road, starting up the final two-mile hill towards home, cars whizzing close, we both started to flag. Isabel kept at it, but she was now slightly behind me. I glanced down repeatedly to see how she was doing. She was plugging along, and so I did too. When we finally reached home, my back aching, I bent down to scratch her ears, massaging her through her thick flowing coat. I looked into her trusting face, and tears of love, gratitude, and joy came. We stumbled our way, together, into the house. We'd done it, together.

—

The day of the marathon, I shivered in the early April morning air, bouncing leg to leg to try to stay warm and to manage my jagged nerves. I wanted to make it all 26.2 miles. My goal: not to walk a single step. As the runners started down the first big hill out of Hopkinton, I turned my mind to my mantras. I had a list of names ready, one focal point for each mile—one person who'd helped me get to the starting line to thank and to reflect on. The names helped, my legs rising in rhythm, lighter when thinking of those who had supported me. The roar of the crowd carried me on, as if I was riding sound. As the miles clicked by, I managed to climb the infamous Heartbreak Hill, thrilled I still felt good. But next came the miles I was most uncertain about. There was so much talk of people "hitting the wall" at mile twenty, unable to continue, and each of these last six miles was taking me to distances I'd never run before.

I forced my mind back to the list of names, sending gratitude to the people who'd helped me, picturing each one in turn. But I began to struggle, having to concentrate all my will to lift each foot, one after the other, my legs aching with the burden. Trying to get up a small rise in the road, not even as high as a curb, felt like an Olympian challenge. Making my way around the final curve to Boylston Street, I was completely focused on the intense effort. As I strained to find the capacity to keep running, I looked ahead and saw the last yards before the finish, and the thought came to me: *I am going to make it.* With that thought, a name that hadn't been on my list burst through the fog of fatigue: *Isabel.* How had I missed her? Without Isabel, I would not have made it to the starting line, let alone to the finish. A sob rose in me as I crossed the blue and yellow line and stumbled forward, a marathoner.

The day after the race, I walked into a meeting at work, one that usually had me cowering. A particular manager regularly flung flaming spears, often at me. But that day, I sat calmly, strangely immune to her barbs. I felt my legs, usually shifting restlessly, quiet on the chair. The limits and pressures that had seemed overwhelming to me had somehow been left behind on the roads and trails I'd covered with Isabel and on the marathon route she had brought me to run.

Isabel had worked her magic. But like me, she was changed by that long run. The next time I put on running shoes and tried to get her to head out with me, she ever so subtly turned from the door, just a slight movement, but a tell: She'd go for a run if I needed her to, but she'd rather not. Isabel was such a giving spirit that I had to watch her carefully. She would do anything she thought I wanted, without reservation. It was all too easy to take advantage of a generosity like that. She was not one to decline an invitation, and reluctantly, I listened. Our shared running days came to an end.

———

Though Isabel wasn't running with me anymore, we found a new adventure to take on together. With my daughter deep into her middle school world and my husband and I living in mostly separate worlds, some space opened for me to find my joy—and my escape. Isabel and I looked to the mountains, where beauty, tranquility, and the intense physicality of strenuous hiking soothed my soul.

I was on a quest to hike the highest summits in New Hampshire, inspired by *Following Atticus*, a memoir by a man who had climbed all those peaks together with his small dog, who was about Isabel's size. I was seized by the idea that Isabel and I could share a similar journey, and as always, she came through. She collected praise and attention on the trails as she soldiered up challenging peaks, and she somehow managed to contain her mad enthusiasm for chasing ground squirrels—mostly. She turned out to be a natural and avid hiker. The first time we went up a big mountain together, Isabel clambered up boulders, scrambling with her huge fluffy paws, accepting a lift from me here and there but mostly managing all on her own. Reaching the top, she made her way to a spot near a rocky outcropping. There she sat, in perfect stillness, gazing out at the horizon, her eyes, like mine, on the layers and layers of mountains, receding to what felt like infinity. The subtle shades of blue, the vastness before us, seemed to captivate her as much as me. She sat, unmoving, for long minutes before we stood to pose for a picture at the summit, Isabel in my arms. Together, we had found a realm, separate from all demands, a profound peace. On every hike, Isabel found her ledge and sat before the ever-unfolding landscape, a tiny Buddha.

We had managed six of the 4,000-foot peaks in New Hampshire together and had our routines pretty well down when one late fall day, we decided to tackle Mount Pierce. We started from the parking lot in the earliest sunlight, a few leaves of muted bronze and gold still clinging to the trees. But as is so often the case in the mountains, the weather was fickle, especially as we climbed higher. We struggled up the trail, and as we neared the summit, where the trees were beginning to give way to exposed rock, we were caught in a sudden squall. Swirling snow blasted us from every direction, stinging our eyes and rapidly soaking us. The snow and wind had such fury that it quickly wiped out our footprints, obscuring the trail. Suddenly, the soft fall day was gone, and there was nothing around us but a wall of white. Panic flooded me— what if we got lost up here, in this wet and blinding snow? I knew how soon hypothermia could set in. I could see that despite the fleece dog jacket covering her body and legs, Isabel was becoming wet, and snow was clumping heavily, in huge balls, on her feet and ears. My breathing came fast as I bent over her, trying to shield her as I scanned around us. Which way? If I chose wrong, Isabel could pay a very steep price, and it would be my fault.

I looked down into her wide eyes, ice collecting on her tan brows. My heart was banging in my chest, and my breath was coming in little gasps of panic. But in Isabel's limpid gaze, I saw nothing but love and nothing but trust. She had no doubt or fear. I tried to breathe more slowly. In, out, in, out. Crouching to block the snow from her, I looked out again at the sea of white around us. Did that one rock look familiar? Had we passed it on our way up to this spot?

In Isabel's loving assurance, I found mine. We started back towards the rock and soon found ourselves protected again by trees, where the snow was lighter, and I could see a faint hint of the trail. As we made our way down, Isabel was encumbered by heavy wet snowballs, and I had to stop every few minutes to break them apart. It was slow going. But we made it down the mountain, soaked but safe, together. As she lay curled in the back seat, the heater blasting and the ice melting from her coat, I smothered her in my arms.

———

In her tenth year, the vet was clear: "She has an enlarged heart, not uncommon in this breed. Medication may help, but not for long." I arrived home from the clinic in a stupor and, clinging to routine, left with Isabel for our evening walk. It was already dark. The blankness of night was a comfort, a protection, holding us. Isabel walked slowly, with great effort. I did not want to strain her heart, that huge heart of hers. I picked her up and carried her, my arms aching, holding her against my chest, my heart breaking with hers.

Isabel and I had summited one inspiring mountain after another, and I had wanted to keep going. But it was obvious Isabel couldn't. I yearned for our shared glory on the peaks, but Isabel didn't seem to regret the adjustment—she came to love our new routine. We shifted our walks to a flat one-mile loop around a local reservoir, which at her pace took about forty minutes. I would stand on the curving path and look back to watch her, waiting for her to catch up. I was restless at first, struggling to adjust to this very different pace, but over time, Isabel drew me into a new rhythm. In her quiet way, she'd shown me how to slow down, how to pause, what it felt like not to rush.

But our walks got shorter and slower. One morning, after struggling to provide the right medication for her enlarged heart, I could see she was not herself, not even her slowed-down self. Battling commuter traffic, I rushed her to the emergency hospital. Isabel immobile at my side, I struggled to speak to the staff. I broke down as I tried to explain. They said they would keep her to run tests to see what was happening to her heart and would call me to discuss options.

I left her there, trying to drive but seeing only the image of her stoic but strained face as I left her behind. Somehow, I made it home. I left the car and had started down the sidewalk from my house to catch the bus to work when my phone buzzed. The veterinarian was somber.

"I'm afraid she's gone."

Isabel had died on the table as they were prepping her for an ultrasound. Her huge heart was her greatest gift, and her undoing.

I lost Isabel not only at that one awful moment, but hundreds of times, each time as if it were the first, hitting me again and again, a fresh swirling wave, sucking me deep into churning water, engulfing me in empty darkness.

I lose her as I stand at the stove making popcorn. I feel her behind me, where she always stood, patiently but expectantly, when I made her favorite snack. I turn to give her a few of the warm, freshly popped pieces only to find my hand hovering in empty space. For ten years I had not eaten popcorn without sharing with Isabel. We would sit on the floor with an overflowing bowl, one piece for me, one for her. But not tonight. Tonight, my hand flutters from open air to my chest.

I lose her washing dishes. I glance left, to her favorite chair, where I would always catch her gaze upon me, her round, soulful brown eyes connecting with mine, her long black feathery ears shining in the light. But the chair where she lay for more than a decade is empty. She is gone, again. I turn to the sink, head bowed, letting the water run, joining the stream of my tears.

I lose her when preparing the shopping list. I hear her strong, deep breath from her special place in the next room, breathing like sighing, the lullaby of our shared life. Hearing her, I look up, for a moment, forgetting again. And then, seeing an empty chair, I gasp. The terrible truth hits as if for the first time: Her breath cannot be.

Isabel had lived close by my side for nearly eleven years; we were connected as if we were one being. My brain refused to grasp that she was gone. Perhaps she wasn't gone, not really. It would be so like her to come to comfort me for losing her. That would be so like my Isabel.

My very cells yearned for her. Writhing, they willed me towards her, wherever she had gone.

I was haunted. There were kind reassurances: "You did all you could" and "These things happen." Yet amid these efforts to salve my wounds, doubt gnawed, corrosive. Did I? Did I do "all I could?" Had I misunderstood the vet, done the wrong thing with medication? Had I been blinded by my own need, pushed her too hard on runs, in the mountains, weakening her heart? That precious life, a soul so pure, a heart so open, and only I to protect her. Did I? The question was torment, unanswered, unanswerable.

If Isabel could have weighed in, I knew what her response would be, "I love you. It's okay." She had never blamed, never judged. Not once. Her gentle, accepting approach to the world had made me think she was vulnerable. So, trusting, so loving, I worried that she could be hurt, so easily—including by me. It was only when she was gone that I could see more clearly that her pure loving acceptance wasn't vulnerability at all. It was her secret superpower. Whatever happened, she had all she wanted: life by my side.

You can't be deserving of love like that. You can only get onto your knees and try to let the grace of it in.

The Perfection of Lovingkindness, in Buddhist teachings, is acting with compassion for all beings and boundlessly wishing that all beings be happy. As with all the Perfections, the practice of lovingkindness offers a path to happiness. By loving unconditionally, we are, as Sylvia Boorstein says, "protected," as Isabel was, "by [our] own lovingness."[5] Isabel shared her abundant love without qualification or limit, with a purity and persistence that held me in a constant embrace. She was, and will always be, my beloved teacher, a small, miraculous, mighty embodiment of the power of perfect lovingkindness.

9

GRACIE – EQUANIMITY

Equilibrium, balance, peace

Movers arrived to extract all that my husband had accumulated in our thirty years of marriage. I didn't want to witness the rending of our shared life. And I was determined to mark this juncture with a gesture tied to my future, not my past. So at fifty-five, I did something I had never done before: I rented a vacation house on my own.

On that warm, sunny August day, my golden retriever, Gracie, and I piled into my aging Subaru and headed north. As I hit the highway, my body vibrated with the old engine, trembling with terror—but also excitement. The wide-open road. The first step into my new life.

I had prepared as if for a siege. A dear friend had agreed to confer with me every night in case I got scared or sad. I had brought enough food and water to survive at least a week without having to find a store. I had books to uplift my spirit and trail maps to guide us. And perhaps most of all, I had Gracie. With her in the backseat, her knowing face intently watching my every move, I did not feel I was heading out on this journey alone. Even though she was still very young, at just a year and a half she had already become my ballast, steadying me, especially now, as we ventured into the unknown.

When Gracie came into my life as an adorable pup of eight weeks, her lustrous, creamy coat glowing as if she were a miniature moon, I was utterly taken by the poise of this small being. Her brown eyes, the color of rich dark tea, were set off by striking black rims and impossibly tiny lashes the color of the lightest toasted toffee. On a quick glance, the impression she gave was of a strikingly beautiful, placid puppy. But the expression in those eyes, even from the start, was intense, keen, observant, carrying the solid force of her.

At the time of her arrival, I had had no idea of the wild seas that lay ahead. But it was almost as if she did, and she knew what her job would need to be. She grounded me from the start. She was an ideal housemate: mild, and seemingly born with good manners. I quickly learned that under her docile exterior lay the steely resolve of a task-master, but her adherence to protocols made puppyhood a breeze. Housetraining? Of course it made sense to take care of business outside. These cues for sit and whatnot? Very simple. Puppy pen in the kitchen? A happy place to rest. Guests squealing and wanting to pet her? She quietly engaged with them all. As for nights, from the first, she slept cuddled quietly next to me, a peaceful, protective presence. She had found her spot on the bed without fuss, avoiding any competition with my little Pomeranian Jasper, who had an undisputed place on a pillow next to me. Despite Jasper's small size, she naturally deferred to him, a deference that came across not as submissiveness, but politeness, a sense of what was proper.

And so, Gracie and I arrived at the rented house overlooking Squam Lake on an August day. We had left the aging Jasper home, and Gracie was, as usual, completely composed and riveted on me, her eyes asking me what was next, making sure I was on track. When we awoke at sunrise after that first night, it was to a mesmerizing flow of oranges and pinks. Perched above the lake, we watched the swirling colors spread across the sky, a spectacle of warmth and energy.

For our hike that day we chose a small mountain, Mount Percival. Gracie didn't need to be on a leash—as always, she stayed right on the trail and right with me. At the top of the mountain, she and I sat together, looking out at the expanse before us. As I gazed from the summit onto the splendor laid out below, Gracie and I were but tiny flecks in a world so rich and exquisite that I felt tears pressing at the corner of my eyes. Here, with the rolling hills and grey-blue water sparkling under a cloudless sky, the mountains shimmering in the distance, their massive forms laid out in an endlessly receding horizon—here, we were folded into beauty and peace. Worries about the future, shame about the past, the scripts that had been looping over and over in my brain, taunting and tormenting me, here, they stopped running.

What was left was gratitude, grace. As I sat on the summit, my arm on my steadfast Gracie, I thought how she had come to me when I didn't expect it, a gift. The breeder had offered her to me when I was deeply grieving the loss of my spaniel Isabel, and I had felt the sheer grace of that gesture. I chose her name to reflect it. But I had no idea how much her name would portend the role she would play in my life or just how much I would need her stability and her tranquil companionship in the years ahead.

There on Mount Percival, her presence was the difference between being alone and being on an adventure with a trusted friend. This was not loneliness. This was shared solitude, shared peace. We sat on the front porch, Gracie at my feet, as one striking sunrise and sunset slid into another, soothing my wounds. We ate our meals and hiked our trails and watched the ever-changing lake, sky, and hills, their massive shapes both gentle and powerful, holding us in their timeless mystery. Gracie's quiet, loyal presence enveloped me, her warmth and watchfulness pushing out fear, grief, and anguish, offering a bulwark as I faced the future. With her, on those hills, I felt peace. And perhaps a hint of something strange: joy.

When we pulled away from the lake for the drive home, Gracie sat alert in the back seat, and my hands were loose and easy on the wheel. Together, we faced the road ahead.

We came back home from Squam Lake to our newest routine, spending each morning at the local park, where Gracie and I had been walking with Jasper. I felt calmer, more grounded from our time in the mountains. I was beginning to feel maybe, just maybe, I could do this thing, this living on my own. I even managed to run the lawn mower myself—an embarrassingly small, but to me significant, triumph. But then, just a few weeks after our trip, another blow came: Jasper died suddenly. I'd made it through the divorce and the health scare and the parenting challenges that summer, but this blow, coming on top of the others—this one took me to the floor. I lay, sadness and despair flowing through me, viscous and paralyzing.

But I had to find a way to stand, for Gracie. I had to be there for her. I forced myself up and out. And by returning to the park after Jasper's loss, I met Jaime. Even when the world had opened in resplendent beauty and peace on top of Mount Percival a few weeks before, such a turn of events was beyond imagining. And yet the reality was better than what I could have dreamed up—or what I felt I could ever deserve. Jaime had come into my life, and he and I had started running regularly together, our version of dating.

One Saturday morning some months after Jasper's death, Jaime and I were running on a trail in a local conservation area with Gracie, as we did every week. We were striding side by side, Gracie a little to our left as we flowed down a hill, a tight threesome. Gracie, as always, was at a strong, smooth trot, her pristine white coat fluttering slightly in the breeze, her mouth parted just a little in that peaceful smile she often had. A woman was coming up the trail from the other direction. She looked up at us, her mouth and eyes wide.

"You three look like a picture in a catalog!" she called out.

Her words caught and carried me, soaring. In this quiet New England forest, people were friendly enough but tended toward the polite and reserved, offering a slight head nod or a swift, "How ya doin'?" So when a passerby shared these words with such a burst of spirit, it seemed like a signal that the connection between Jaime, Gracie, and me was strong enough to be apparent to a stranger. That moment with them helped me yield to the growing trust I had: The three of us, we belonged together. Gracie's sweet, reliable presence was a core part of the package.

She was a connecting force: She, along with Jasper, was the reason I'd met Jaime. Divorce had left me holed up inside myself, feeling like a wounded failure, but as our life took on its new, open contours, I found the confidence to reach out into the world again with Gracie at my side. Gracie had passed her therapy dog evaluation, and she and I began regularly visiting a hospital's inpatient psychiatric unit, where the residents gathered in a common room, chairs circled on thin gray carpet, and Gracie interacted with each person in turn. One day, a woman, Cathy, whom we hadn't seen before, joined the group. She seemed a bit younger than many of the other residents, her straight, silver-blond hair pulled back in a loose ponytail. She sat in a wheelchair, petting Gracie, and we talked casually back and forth.

"She's beautiful. She reminds me so much of a dog I had growing up," Cathy said. Her hands and eyes were fully on Gracie. Her face was lined, but her gray-blue eyes were soft as she gazed down at Gracie, whose head rested lightly against her leg. Talking with this woman was like being out for tea with a friend, and I felt real ease and connection between her and Gracie.

After our visit, the coordinator escorted us out to the elevator and stopped in front of the doors. She looked up at me, her eyes holding mine. "That was amazing," she said. "Cathy is typically catatonic. She doesn't respond to or speak with anyone."

I tried to take in what she was saying. Cathy, the woman who had been chatting with us like old friends? Normally unresponsive, unreachable? I was stunned.

The coordinator went on, speaking rapidly, her eyes intense. "I ran to get the staff psychiatrist; I wanted her to witness the transformation. It was incredible. I didn't think she'd believe it if she didn't see it."

I was thrilled and humbled by how Gracie, with her steadfast, unruffled presence, could reach people and bring them peace, even if for just a few minutes. Every time she worked her magic, the experience took me out of my own haunted mind by bringing me into communion with others. The healing bonds blended into daily life, sustaining and stabilizing me.

These visits were good for both of us, and Gracie and I began visiting a youth vocational program, which aimed to help young people facing challenges on the path to independent adulthood. One young woman, June, had recently arrived in the United States, bearing the burdens of significant trauma. She came from a culture where dogs were not pets. June had learned a bit of English, but on our initial visits, she stood apart, her tall, thin frame glued to the wall, her eyes warily on Gracie. As the weeks passed, and she saw the dog quietly engaging with others, June began to stand nearer to Gracie, watching her closely. After several visits, she tried what she had seen others do—she held out her hand so Gracie could place her paw there. When Gracie responded and their hands touched, June smiled so broadly that her eyes crinkled at the corners, and, releasing Gracie's paw, she bounced with glee.

The next time we visited, June approached us and did something she'd never done before. She threw herself down on the rug right next to Gracie, and in moments, was lying on the floor with her, laughing. Gracie, usually peaceful rather than playful, bowed in classic dog fashion, paws outstretched, rump in the air, and with tail wagging, she began rolling alongside June. I stood frozen, watching their shared delight, so unimaginable just a few weeks before. But not long after that, we learned that June was taking a big step, moving to a group home and leaving the program. When we said goodbye, June stroked Gracie. She looked up at me. "Gracie visit?" she asked.

This young woman, who had been raised to consider dogs filthy and threatening, who had lived through terribly wounding experiences, had opened her heart to Gracie. Gracie had become her friend, a friend she wanted to see at her new home. I left that day with my heart full, my steps sure. Together, in her peaceful, tempered presence, we were making connections of the heart that neither of us could foster alone. Sharing in these moments made me feel I could rejoin humanity, that despite my failings and flaws, despite not being able to sustain my closest relationship, my marriage, I could still share love in the world.

———

And so I made my way forward, making a new life with Gracie by my side. By the time I was turning sixty, she and Jaime and I were a well-established family, having shared many miles together. Jaime and I had taken up a half-marathon quest—one race in every New England state in one year—and I'd decided to try a half marathon on a trail. The day of the race, I found the route heavy, slow going, the narrow trail muddy and wet in the transition to spring. Despite the conditions, I rejoiced in being in the woods with other runners. By the end, though, I struggled to take even a single step. I stumbled into the parking lot and slumped over onto the grass, completely spent, so stiff I was reluctant to try to get up.

The next day one of my hips was so tight I had to stretch my leg out straight behind me in order to reach anything on the floor, and tying my shoes was nearly beyond my ability. I consulted my physical therapist, who suggested an X-ray, and within days I found myself with a startling diagnosis: osteoarthritis in my hip. At the initial consult with an orthopedic specialist, she looked at me somberly and told me to go home, and "try to be as active as you can. When you can't walk around the block any more, come back. That's when it'll be time to consider a hip replacement."

In a matter of a few weeks, I had gone from being an avid long-distance runner to someone unable to tie my shoes or go for walk without ending up in agony. I wasn't just reeling from the shock, I was bereft. Running—especially with Gracie and Jaime—was not just exercise, it was my deepest source of peace and joy. It was how I had fed and replenished my spirit since I was sixteen. Scrambling to find some way out of this predicament, I heard about a surgeon who supported his hip replacement patients in getting back to running after surgery, and I went to see him as soon as I could.

His assessment was clear: end-stage osteoarthritis. "You're going to need a new hip. You can wait, or you can have the surgery now."

"So if I wait, I'll just be back here in a year, weaker and more out of shape, still needing the same surgery?"

"That's the situation. But with the surgery, you'll be able to get back to all your activities."

My choice was clear. I didn't just want to run, I *had* to run. "I'm in," I told him. I got on a waitlist, and just a few months from diagnosis, I had a new hip.

The dark winter night when I came home from the hospital, Gracie—usually relentless about schedules and routines—seemed to understand immediately that it was a time to pull inward. I was using crutches and was agonizingly slow in moving about the house. It was a week before I took the single step down onto our deck and finally felt the air again, a whiff of a frigid, fresh breeze that was like being on a mountaintop. I inched carefully around the house, trying not to bang my leg, or worse, fall. I had awakened from the surgery in euphoria; as I lay in the recovery room babbling thanks, my anesthesiologist smiled at me and said "Yeah, that's the drugs talking." But that wild relief had faded as the pain surged, and my mind took hold of a thought I didn't dare speak: *What if this leg doesn't heal?* I tried not to dwell in my fear, but the evidence of the change wrought in my body was branded onto my brain. When I closed my eyes, I could see the post-surgical X-ray with the sharp contours of a foreign object—a crisp hammer glowing inside my femur, a cup screwed neatly in place at the top—a bionic hip.

Gracie didn't get caught in anxiety as I did. She fluidly changed gears. Instead of nudging me with her usual restless and persistent whines when it was time for her morning walk, she lay quietly near me. She didn't seem to notice that we weren't going out, though she went eagerly with the dog walker. She never bumped me, never touched my wounded leg when we were sleeping. I knew I could rely on her completely. I clung to her as to a rope that would pull me from this sea of fear.

It was weeks before I could drive or feel confident enough to take even the smallest walk with Gracie. Our first trip out was to her favorite place, the local reservoir. It was late winter, a day that was turning toward spring. I gingerly extracted myself from the car and opened the back door for Gracie. I walked slowly, painstakingly, carefully leaning on two hiking poles. I felt I'd aged several decades since the last time we'd been on this wide dirt trail where I usually ran or strode rapidly next to the large pond. I braced myself, afraid that a dog or person would bump into me. But as I inched along drinking in the cool air, the relief and joy of walking again without pain made me feel whole. Gracie, out with me for the first time in weeks, seemed to sense what was needed. She walked quietly, a few paces to my left as we made our way along the path, her stable presence once again a stronghold against everything that lay ahead.

Gracie had been supporting me for a decade, pulling me from despair back into connection, helping me heal in spirit and in body, providing a solid base from which I could open up and embrace a new and happy life. But around her tenth birthday, her age began to show. She started to turn away from the door when I brought out the leash for running. And on therapy dog visits I could see that her interest and capacity for that kind of sustained engagement had waned. So Gracie retired as a runner and as a therapy dog. The passing of these partnerships was poignant, not only because of the joy we had shared but also because our close teamwork was the foundation for building a life more loving and beautiful than I'd ever dared dream.

Yet Gracie's partnership with me hasn't ended, it's just entered a new phase. Her latest project to support me has been her vigilant work training our puppy, Leo. His transgressions are many—while Gracie was born a rule follower, Leo has not yet grasped the idea of a rule—but Gracie has been my reliable partner as always, working diligently to get Leo in line. A decade after naming her, I see it: Her name exquisitely captures not just the gift of how unexpectedly she came to heal me but what she has offered every day since. Pure grace.

In Buddhist teachings, the heart quality of equanimity can be thought of as standing strong and steady in the face of life's inevitable flow of changes and challenges, of not losing balance by grasping towards what one wants, or by pushing away what one doesn't. Equanimity is climbing a mountain and seeing everything clearly, from a little distance, without being caught up in judgment, fear, or even hope—hope that things will go a certain way. It is staying steady when the world unexpectedly shifts. Gracie has brought me this equanimity. She has been my ballast in the winds of life, a steadying force, guiding me toward stable ground, a foothold enabling me to reach out with open arms to create a new life. She's helped me find the balance that makes it possible to move forward, head up, step by step, toward all life can hold.

10

LEO – DETERMINATION

Persevering to find a compassionate path

My young golden retriever Leo was just off the trail, running not far from me as I drew in the moist cool air of early spring. There was nothing that brought me more happiness than running in the woods with Leo. His speed and athleticism, his unadulterated joy, pulled me along as if I were being carried on a wave, buoyant. Then, suddenly, a whining cry from him broke our rhythm.

There was only one thing that would make Leo call out like that: the fresh trail of a wild creature. I watched in dread as his creamy form shot up and over a hill. Given how fast and far he was running, he was almost assuredly chasing a deer. In the time it took me to stop, scan for him, and take a single ragged breath, he was gone, out of sight and out of sound.

The woods were part of a larger tract of open land, but Leo was very fast, and I knew that a highway was only a mile or so away in the direction he was heading. My breaths came rapidly, high in my chest, as I began walking up the hill, shouting for Leo.

I tried to remember the advice I had read about losing a dog in the woods: Stay where you last saw your dog; call so they can hear where you are. I struggled to focus, but my pulse fluttered like that of a trapped hamster, and I could not draw enough air, my body trembling with panic. In other situations, Leo's recall was perfect. Here, I called for Leo over and over, trying to sound calm and happy, so he would be more likely to come to me. But the woods around me stayed still and silent, as if life itself had been suspended. Desperate, I tried to reach my partner, Jaime, calling and texting once, then dozens of times, more and more frantically. There was no response.

My older golden, Gracie, stayed quietly near me, glancing up every so often, her brow wrinkled. I put my hand on her. "It's going to be okay. We're going to find him."

As I paced, Gracie settled onto a patch of leaves, her eyes following me up and down the trail as I strode up and back, peering through the trees for any movement, calling for Leo. I caught sight of a runner coming along the trail, a dog happily following.

"Have you seen a dog that looks like this one?" I called out, pointing to Gracie.

The man slowed his pace, then stopped. "You lost one?"

I nodded.

"Give me your phone number and I will call you if I see him."

I nodded, my throat almost too tight to speak, and choked out my number, which he entered into his phone. He caught my eye, his face serious, and he spoke softly. "It'll be okay." Then he turned and continued down the trail and around a curve. Alone again, I stared at the spot where he had disappeared, but the trembling in my arms and hands eased a little bit just from knowing that another person was involved in finding Leo, no matter how loosely.

A dog walker passed, and I called out again, asking if he'd seen a white dog. I was relieved when he paused. "I am so sorry," he said. "The same thing has happened with my dog, and it's so scary. He'll come back."

The willingness of strangers to take in my fear, to share my burden, however briefly, was like being held with great tenderness. But as each of these kind people moved on down the trail, I was left pacing on my own, up and down the hill, calling, and all the while pushing back the terrible thought that I had lost my dearest, most beloved boy. And it was my fault.

———

Jaime and I had brought Leo home when he was eight weeks old—one of the many "pandemic puppies" welcomed because of the new flexibility of remote work. I was working from home and had seized the chance to find a puppy, one that I hoped would be a companion for me and Jaime and our dog, Gracie, and who would join me in two particular activities: trail running and therapy dog visits.

The search for a breeder led Jaime and me to a small farm in the middle of the state, to a no-nonsense woman who was adeptly managing young children, a herd of alpacas, and a breeding and showing program for golden retrievers as well. We were thrilled when she called in response to our application to tell us that there was a puppy available in her current litter, born a few days before, if we wanted one. She also told us why she was making a puppy available to us. "My approach is not first-come-first-served. We are looking for a match. My twelve-year-old daughter liked that you are involved with therapy dog volunteering. That's why we picked you."

She told us how she would use a standard puppy aptitude test to find the best fit for us, including assessing potential as a therapy dog. She explained that she bred carefully for health, longevity, conformation, and temperament. I was feeling more certain and more excited with every word.

"I also breed for hunting instinct," she said.

The phrase stood out, given my suburban life. My aim was to go out into the world with my dog to visit people, not to stalk game. When I asked what she meant, the breeder explained that hunting was a core part of the golden retriever's heritage and that she was committed to perpetuating all the qualities the breed has had from the beginning. Her philosophy was clear and coherent. She saw no incompatibility with the kind of personality we were looking for and was willing to work to find a match for us in the litter. I thought of how avidly some of my other dogs had chased squirrels. That hadn't changed their ability to be therapy dogs. I set my questions aside.

I spoke with the breeder again when the puppies were seven weeks old, old enough to have the temperament assessment. The whole litter had scored well—neither too bold nor too meek. Either extreme, she explained, could make the dog more difficult to train and live with. But she was not satisfied that she had enough information to choose which of two males in the litter would be more likely to be a good fit for therapy dog visits, which one was the most outgoing with people and internally motivated to engage with them. She told us she had devised her own additional, informal test to determine which of the two males showed the most promise and thus should be matched with us.

"The one we're calling Big Boy is the winner," she told us. "He was the puppy who persisted the longest in following my five-year-old around, trying to play with him, no matter how annoying he got!"

I laughed about this unique "annoying kindergartner" assessment but also took her report seriously, thrilled she had taken extra steps to identify the puppy most likely to enjoy therapy dog visits.

Just a few days later, we met the breeder at her log cabin home, all of us wearing masks to protect against COVID-19. Standing straight and tall, long blond hair falling down her back, her bearing was a reassuring combination of brisk efficiency and warmth—earthy and professional. We eagerly signed paperwork and met her adult dogs. Then she brought out our puppy, placing him on the kitchen floor. I sank to my knees, immediately entranced by the solid, eager, curious pup. He calmly wandered over to Jaime and me in turn, wagging and sniffing, his dark brown eyes chocolate against his fluffy coat, the color of marshmallow fluff. I could hardly believe he was real, and all I wanted to do was hug him to me and run home with him. As we gathered the bag of dog food and the papers to leave, the breeder asked casually if we'd named our pup yet. We told her we had some ideas but were waiting to see what would fit him. She smiled and then caught my eyes and held them.

"Be careful what you name him. He'll become whatever you call him."

After getting to know our puppy for a day or so, we quickly decided upon his name: Leo. The direct meaning of the name, lion, suited his confidence, strength, and fascination with chasing wild creatures like our backyard squirrels. But the almost lyrical softness of the name also fit, for this pup was unfailingly sweet and affectionate, running to us and rubbing his compact muscular body against our legs, moaning with pleasure. Our puppy was a remarkable mix of the tame and the untamed. And as the breeder had predicted, his name came to suit him all too well.

———

Late one night when Leo was just eleven weeks old, he scratched at the door asking to go out, and I pulled myself out of bed and stumbled outside into the moonlight so he could pee. As I followed him around the yard, foggy with sleep, I saw him snatch at something from the dirt near a rock wall. I could not be sure, but my mind registered the form of a tiny rabbit. I bent closer and saw that Leo was gulping something down. I stood, my body frozen and my mind muddled. Certainly, a puppy less than three months old could not chase, catch, and consume a tiny, adorable creature in seconds, right in front of me? Surely, I had not seen my adorable, loving, sweet puppy dispatch a baby bunny as efficiently as a lion in the wild?

As the weeks went on, Leo's hunting prowess became ever more apparent. My spaniel Isabel had been fixated on squirrels and chipmunks, and Gracie was extremely keen to watch and dart briefly after rabbits. But neither of them had the focus, drive, or ability that Leo had. Leo, so affable, outgoing, gentle, and engaging with people, had another gear when he was outside in the woods. A switch flipped, and his drive to follow a scent, then catch and dispatch small creatures took over. The beauty of his movement through the woods and his intense athleticism and focus were as compelling to watch as an episode on the Nature Channel. But the results tore at me. Death had never been part of my experience in these peaceful suburban woods before.

Leo's delight meant injury not only for other creatures but for the landscape, and sometimes for him. He would get so excited about a ground squirrel that he would dig a huge hole in seconds; he would pull up a small sapling by the roots, grasping and wrenching the trunk in his strong jaws. He would thrust his head deep into any fallen, rotting log, even if he ripped himself open with the effort, once ending up with an abscess on his head the size of a baseball. When hunting, it was as if he entered a trance. Nothing mattered but the chase.

—

On that day in the woods after Leo ran off, as I traced the route up and down the area nearest where I had last seen him, I pictured him in that hypnotized state, running wild after some creature. Gracie was following at my side. Ever my constant, calm supporter, I could see even she was starting to be more subdued about this strange change in routine, her head hanging a little low and her eyes penetrating, questioning, when she glanced at me. I tried to talk to her in an upbeat, light voice, but it sounded forced, even to my own ears.

"We'll find him. He'll come back." I played the phrases on a loop, an incantation to keep from collapsing.

I checked my phone, again. I looked at my watch, again. Twenty minutes, thirty... fifty. By now Leo could have been hit by a car or have run so far away that he'd be gone for good. A dog who had been lost in these very woods a few years back, despite massive efforts, was never found. I started slowly back down the trail from the way we'd come, thinking that he could follow our scent trail back to the car. I clutched my phone in one hand, Gracie's leash in the other. My body taut and aching, I tried to imagine how I could possibly share the news with Jaime.

After a few yards, I stopped abruptly, every sense strained. Had I heard movement in the woods? Or was I imagining it? I froze, listened, and scanned the forest. And there he was. Leo, running out of the woods, tongue extended and flopping, sides heaving, eyes alight, looking as if he'd just had the best time of his life. I gasped and folded over, limp.

I drew huge gulping breaths, and I willed myself to remember and use the advice I'd read. Don't scold. Don't immediately grab him and put the leash on him. Praise him for coming back. I succeeded in managing two of these. But I could not keep myself from attaching his leash while giving him a huge handful of treats as a reward for returning to me. As I watched Leo gobble up the goodies, relief and gratitude flooded me. I had my boy back, my beloved, sweet, wild spirit. He looked up at me, happy and relaxed, his eyes sparkling, ready for the next adventure.

———

After that terrifying episode in the woods, I kept Leo on a leash for more than a year. I was afraid of losing him again, possibly forever. But I could not shake a sense of guilt. I was keeping him from his passion: running free in the woods, hunting. As a trail runner myself, I knew how running could be a wellspring of joy, creativity, and peace. I didn't want to deprive Leo of his version of that. But no matter how many times I turned the problem over in my mind, I couldn't devise a plan for how to give Leo his happiness—and also keep him safe. As the months wore on, I felt not so much his partner as his captor.

I consulted trainers, I read books, I talked to every friendly dog walker I saw, especially those with hunting dogs. Every piece of information helped, but none of their suggestions felt quite right for me and Leo. One person advocated letting a dog get lost; they'd learn to come back. Many others were using electronic collars, the ones that could deliver a shock, and they insisted their dog had never been hurt, only helped. Other people were sporting expensive GPS equipment, but with a tracking radius that would only locate Leo if he were nearby, and only if he didn't go in the water. And I'd still have to catch him.

Then, through a dog-related group on social media, I stumbled on a different approach—a running sport Leo and I could do together: canine cross country, or cani-cross. When I saw dozens of pictures of happy people running with dogs like Leo, I jumped into action, ordering a padded harness designed for pulling, similar to a sled dog harness, and a stretchy bungee leash that attached to a belt around my waist. With this gear, Leo and I went back to the big woods to run together.

Running with him connected to me, a sense of rightness suffused me. It was so deep and pure, it felt primal. It was as if my body was enacting an ancient ritual my ancestors from 10,000 years ago had perfected and passed on to me. He and I were one, joined together with each other, in harmony. We'd gone from being a crazy pair, an old woman dragged by a big unruly dog, to a sporty team, in sync with one another. And Leo got to have his run in the woods—not as fast as he'd like, but at least he was running. For a few blissful weeks, I thought I had finally found a solution.

But one day, when Leo and I were running together on a wide trail, our legs moving smoothly in shared, joyful rhythm, he suddenly bolted left, into the trees, towards open water. His powerful surge jerked me off the trail. I found myself careening headfirst towards a tree, at the mercy of Leo. He was two-thirds my weight and all muscle. Propelled forcibly by the leash at my waist towards the huge tree trunk, I screamed, a ragged, guttural plea.

Instinctively, I put my arms out, but my chest still smashed into the rough bark. I stood panting, my body quivering with the shock and effort, one arm grasping the tree, every fiber straining to hold Leo back. He was pulling intensely, his nose pressed into the pine needles, his lips quivering as they drew in the scent, utterly absorbed in his hunt. I struggled to hold him, frantic with the effort to contain him, not to lose him yet again, and not to be injured in trying. It was just a year and a half after my hip replacement surgery, and I was still quite worried about bumps and falls.

I wanted to throttle Leo. But I also wanted to just let go. To drop to the soft pine needles, to relinquish the relentless struggle to invent a life Leo and I could share, a partnership of joy, love, and happiness. What was wrong with me that I could not provide this sweet, smart, loving dog what he needed, his simple pleasures, without endangering one of us?

I yanked Leo to me, grabbed his harness, and collapsed to my knees next to him. He turned from his pursuit, and looked up at me quizzically, as if noticing for the first time that I was there. I looked into his shining brown eyes, so full of light and love, entirely without calculation or malice. I slumped across his back, burying my face in his creamy fur, my throat tight and aching. I had failed, again, at finding us a path together as a team. I had shown, again, that I was not worthy of this magnificent dog.

When I got home, I was still raw enough to break into sobs when I tried to tell Jaime what had happened. "Leo's perfect, he's glorious, he's the best puppy possible." I paused and tried to control my breath, to find the courage to share the awful truth. "And I can't meet his needs."

Leo had joyfully greeted Jaime and was lapping a full bowl of water. I slumped into a chair, my hands over my face. I'd been entrusted with this remarkable dog, a dog I loved like no other, whose affectionate spirit I admired and cherished, but I could not give him what it seemed he most desired—the freedom to hunt. Not without endangering one of us.

——

I read up again on those "e-collars," but the use of fear and pain to train a dog felt like a boundary I was not willing to cross, not again, not as I had with Gizmo. The wrenching experiences I had using force with Gizmo had left me with guilt and shame that still haunted me. As I wrestled daily with how to give Leo a happy life, two questions persisted about this solution so many had chosen: Would I want to be trained by being shocked when I made a mistake? Would I use an electric shock to teach a child? No matter how many times I asked myself these questions, the answer was always the same: no.

I talked with people I knew and respected, I attended webinars, I consulted Leo's breeder and just about every person I saw on the trails who was using one of these collars. Many said they never used the shock, only the vibrate setting, or they had needed to use the shock only once, and then their dog was transformed. They said their life together was now one of freedom and joy, and the happy, responsive dogs by their sides bore testament to their words. I couldn't deny their stories, and I dug deep to try to find the right path. Didn't I need to be open minded, to be sure I explored every option for Leo? I inched closer to the idea that perhaps the shock collar was a reasonable trade-off, a way to give Leo his freedom, safely. Yet I held back. I'd seen people make mistakes with these collars, including one Saint Bernard I witnessed screaming and contorting in pain after being shocked. And I'd read there were risks, too, for sensitive dogs like Leo, who, despite his bold chases, reacted strongly to having even the smallest fly on his back.

The decision was complicated by another factor: Leo's voracious appetite. On two occasions when I'd felt guilty for keeping him on the leash and let him run free in the woods, he ended up in the emergency room, having swallowed an object that blocked his digestive system. In one case, the vet had to perform emergency surgery to save his life, extracting an object—perhaps a corncob—that he had gulped down when exploring the woods on his own. An e-collar could not prevent that.

I turned the problem over and over, a rough stone with no smooth surface to land on. It tumbled ceaselessly in my mind for months. Then, finally, one day the tumbling stopped. I knew. I knew I couldn't risk the electronic collar. I couldn't risk losing Leo's trust, I couldn't risk teaching him fear or breaking his optimistic, cheerful, carefree spirit. And I knew that if I had learned anything from my tortured years with Gizmo, if I was to atone in any way for my cruel actions, it was finally clear: I would not intentionally inflict pain on a dog again. And I knew I had to take an approach that would keep him safe from ingesting another object and needing another abdominal surgery, risking his life. And I knew the most difficult thing: I had to make my own call, knowing that whatever I chose, I would profoundly affect another being.

———

Despite my torment over how to give Leo the chance to run free, I could always see that there was much more to him than his wish to dash in the woods. There had always been two sides of Leo, and just as prominent in his personality was his keen, genuine interest in people. On his puppy playdates, he wanted to meet the person before the dog. He refused to pass the school crossing guard at the corner or the mailman without checking in with them. Everyone was a new best friend.

One day was particularly revealing of Leo's character. I had severe vertigo and was very ill, lying on the bathroom floor, a retching mess, and I needed to make my way to the bedroom down the hall. Pulling a fleece blanket over my back, I began to crawl. As I dragged myself, I felt Leo's solid, warm body come under the blanket and begin to creep beside me, escorting me to the bedroom. I felt him next to me, his strength and his care replenishing and reassuring. He was determined to support me even though he had never, not even once, gone willingly under any blanket; his body temperature was such that he constantly sought ways to cool himself. And he had never adopted such a slow, unnatural pace. Leo's presence under my blanket was uncomfortable for him—a generous, altruistic, completely voluntary act, to help me. I felt his love pass into my tormented body, a powerful healing force.

Jaime and I had always seen Leo's empathy and innate desire to share his love, and this experience when I was sick raised my hopes that he might still be able to be the therapy dog partner I'd wanted. Leo's drive and tendency to get overstimulated—as I'd seen so often in the woods—suggested how things might go awry. But having felt his healing power so personally and powerfully, I knew I desperately wanted to try. When he was about fourteen months old, I signed him up for a therapy dog workshop. I thought, or at least hoped, he was ready.

The day of the workshop, Leo and I finally arrived at the small church where the therapy dog evaluation was to be held just moments before the workshop was to begin. We'd been stuck in traffic, and I was as tense as a tuned guitar string, distressed that my plan to give Leo plenty of time to meet the other dogs and adjust to this new place had fallen apart.

We darted into the building and hesitated at the threshold of the meeting room, where seven dogs were lying quietly in a circle next to their people. There was only one chair left, and it was on the other side of the room.

As we cut across to it, Leo twisted first one way and then the other, checking out the dogs. A booming bark came from deep in his chest, his muscles rippling with the effort. I pulled his leash closer to me, strode forward, and dropped into the chair, my breath coming fast.

The instructor was speaking, but my attention was on Leo. He shifted about and began to whine. It was not his endearing "I want to be your best friend" song, but his edgy "I need to move!" signal. I dug around in the big canvas bag I'd brought, pulled out a chew toy, and tried to get him interested in it. He took it in his mouth briefly, then dropped it. I tried the silent cues that he and I had practiced for months, gestures for "watch me" and "touch" to redirect him. He briefly held my gaze but then returned to his insistent cry.

A wave of sickening heat surged from my gut, burning its way up into my face. I glanced up and caught the stark look of a woman, her calm yellow Lab at her side. In another chair, a woman sat next to her Irish setter who lay, head down, tail tucked, ears perked and, like the woman, peering sideways at Leo and at me. Their eyes bore into me, steely points of judgment.

I had been preparing for this moment since Leo was eight weeks old. And now I sat, an experienced therapy dog teacher and volunteer, miserably unable to manage my own overstimulated, frustrated dog. A class I would usually be teaching was bearing witness to my failure.

The instructor was straining to speak over Leo's whining. My mind emptied of everything but a single aim: ending this humiliation. I stood, Leo looking up at me expectantly, finally silent. The instructor paused, glancing in my direction.

"It seems Leo and I have been here to make the rest of you look good," I said, my lips tightly stretched in an effort at a smile. I hitched my bag higher over one shoulder, grabbed Leo's leash tighter to my side, and fled.

It took time for the sting to fade, but when it eased, I doubled down on our preparation, working with Leo at home, on walks, and in formal classes. I took him to stimulating environments, like Home Depot and other dog-friendly stores, hoping to give him more experience regulating himself in new situations. I focused on developing more communication between us, including a new gesture to request that he stop barking. We continued our efforts to meet people of all kinds, in many contexts, which Leo always loved. And we kept up our canicross running, trying to be sure he had an outlet for his wild side while keeping him safe.

A year after our disaster in the workshop, Leo had matured a bit and was better prepared, I hoped, for another attempt at therapy dog certification. This time, as we sat in the circle at the evaluation, Leo was a bit wiggly, but he was quiet. I practiced breathing in and out, slowly and deeply, working to stifle my own anxieties. In the final stage of the test, when the instructor played the role of a person we were visiting, Leo leaned in, smiled his endearing grin, and danced back and forth, rubbing against her with happiness, his long, feathered tail swishing broadly. He was wriggling, he was lively, and he was completely loving and engaged. The instructor smiled. We had made it, and my wild, wonderful Leo was a therapy dog. As the others chatted and posed for pictures, I didn't press Leo for more. I bolted, our certificate clutched in hand.

———

Almost immediately after we were approved as a team, a request came from an elementary school that needed therapy dogs for a brand new program. I reached out and said I was very interested but that Leo was a new therapy dog, young and excitable, who might bark on a first visit.

That was okay, the counselor said. We arranged to have a short first meeting with staff only so Leo could get used to the school. Leo slid on the linoleum, which made him nervous, and he barked with excitement a couple of times. But he responded to the "no bark" signal we'd worked on and was eager to engage with everyone he met, squinting with pleasure as they stroked and praised him. After the visit, the counselor told me that she and the staff had felt Leo's "loving spirit." They wanted him back.

The counselor selected students for the new program who were grappling with extra issues, whether academic, emotional, or social. Many had difficulties in the classroom, and the plan was to meet with each of them individually outside of that setting, in the counselor's office. Leo made friends with every one of the students right away. He greeted them, his tail wagging softly, brushing up against them, doing his Leo dance of joy.

One day a new student, Sam, joined us for the first time. His huge brown eyes grew even wider when he saw Leo. He came up by Leo's side and began petting his ears and neck and back, smiling. Leo began his leaning, twisting dance of greeting. He rubbed one side along Sam's legs and stomach, then turned and repeated the same on his other side. His thick tail was moving slowly side to side, his mouth partway open in a Leo smile. As Sam continued to pet him, Leo began his throaty, moaning song, his expression of sheer happiness, reserved for being with a special friend.

I explained that Leo could find a hidden toy or do things like Sit and Shake. "He can also play basketball."

At this, Sam's big bright eyes lit up. "Basketball? Yes!" He held the ball out so Leo could push it through a low basketball hoop. "Wow!" he said. "I want Leo to do a slam dunk!"

This wasn't something Leo had done before, and I pictured all the joy and excitement draining out of Sam's face if Leo didn't succeed.

"Leo's never done a slam dunk," I said, "but let's see if we can teach him!"

After a few rounds of Sam holding the ball out farther and encouraging Leo to rush up towards the basket with a bit more verve, Leo thrust his muzzle with such strength that the ball blasted through the basket.

"It's a slam dunk!" Sam and I shouted together. Spontaneously, we began to dance around the room, Leo's tail swishing.

I told Sam he was such a great trainer and partner for Leo. When the counselor came in to take Sam back to his class, he told her, grinning, "I taught Leo to do a slam dunk!"

The counselor smiled and asked Sam if he'd like to keep on seeing Leo. Sam bent over Leo's neck, his arms around Leo's shoulders, and he closed his eyes briefly. Then he looked up. "YES!" When he left the room, he was bouncing.

———

When Leo first met another student, Maddie, she was very natural with him, despite his weighing at least as much as she did. She scratched his ears, and he snuffled against her chest. "I keep telling my mother I want a dog," she said, her voice hesitant, quiet.

Maddie enjoyed many of Leo's standard games—she hid a skunk toy for him to find by scent and played his version of bowling. But she was particularly drawn to the big, round recordable buttons that played back when one of them was pressed—whether by a person, or in this case, a paw. I'd taught Leo to tap a button with his paw, any one of his choosing. I'd started out recording simple "yes" and "no" responses on the buttons so the kids could ask Leo questions, but the students quickly devised many other ways to engage with him through the buttons. Maddie's idea was particularly novel.

"Let's do math with Leo," she said, smiling quietly. She recorded two of the buttons, making one say "four" and the other "ten." She placed the buttons in front of Leo, who was sitting but leaning towards the buttons, eager for the game.

"Leo," she asked, looking into his eyes, "What's two times two?"

I repeated the question, waving my hand across the buttons, trying not to direct Leo in any way. He tapped his paw on the right-hand button. "Four," came the recorded response.

Maddie was thrilled. "That's right, Leo!" Then, "Leo, what's five plus five?"

This time he pressed the button on the left. "Ten," came the voice.

Maddie and I cheered. Leo answered two more questions correctly, missing only one. Maddie was enchanted. "Leo knows math!"

We grinned at each other. "What a great idea you had to use the buttons for math!" I said. Whether Leo had *really* done math didn't seem to matter. That mystery seemed part of the game.

We ended the session with Maddie reading to Leo. Circled together in a small playhouse, Leo curled at her feet, she read him a story. Maddie usually struggled with reading and sometimes stuttered in her speech. But in Leo's presence, her words came smooth and clear.

———

Watching Leo with these students every week, seeing their shared joy, I am drawn into a loving connection that leaves no room for the cynicism and fear that can surround us in this world. When Leo and I are with the students, we enter a simple circle of love. The "reset" that the counselor says students receive from these visits doesn't affect only them. Every time, I, too, feel a fresh start with peace in my heart.

There were doubters, me among them. So many times, it was difficult to see my sweet but exuberant Leo, the masterful hunter, becoming a therapy dog. But there has been one constant: Leo's heart, his innate joy in meeting and engaging with people. His caring spirit has been unmistakable from the beginning, emerging clearly through his soft almond eyes. A visiting friend who was patiently tolerating Leo's insistent wish to be near her and engage with her looked at him, smiling. "What he says with those eyes! He is seeing so far into me!" She has not been the only one who has felt it. When Leo looks into your eyes, his loving spirit fuses with your own. He is seeking a bond, nothing else, and his drive to connect is as strong as his drive to hunt. With determination, we've found ways for him to express both.

One recent morning, just after five a.m., Leo stretched out one big paw and placed it quietly on my chest, as he usually does. His warm spirit and patient affection touches my heart anew. We rise and head out, linked together, running on the trails as the full moon glows, an owl serenades, and the sun begins to rise. As we run, Leo pulls a little toward four deer, their white tails bobbing. I adjust pressure on the leash to direct him, and we run fluidly together, a team. I look down and see him, his ears up, tail out, tongue hanging loose. I see my boy, my Leo, happy.

In Buddhist teachings, the Perfection of Determination is persisting in the face of confusion, being tenacious in the effort to seek clarity. Determination requires careful discernment and continued striving. It is about persevering to find a compassionate path that will benefit others and yield peace of mind.

I have needed to dig deep for the sustained determination to understand Leo and to stay committed to finding a compassionate path for him where he can express both sides of his personality. That path was elusive. There were many times when I felt despair and wanted to give up. But there was Leo, pulling me back with his loving spirit and natural, eager joy for life. I could not fail him by repeating my own mistakes of the past, and I could not let him down. It took years, but we have worked our way to finding joy together, ways we can express our desires and feed our spirits, together. The balance we have most likely won't be a final solution. I expect Leo and I will be partners in a constantly shifting dance. But I have faith now that I can keep finding a balance point between safety and risk, between constraint and freedom, that I can find a compassionate path for my splendid boy—and for me. My ongoing dance with Leo is a precious gift, a gift of love, of joy, of communion. I embrace the dance in Leo's honor and in honor of all my dear dogs.

EPILOGUE

Living so closely with my dogs, bathed in the healing light of their love, companionship, and acceptance, through the joys and the struggles, the successes and the failures, I've found my way farther down the path to happiness. Everything they've taught me in our shared life has ultimately brought joy. From them, I've learned how to hold on but also how to let go. How to be brave enough to stand in the light of truth. What it looks like to be loyal, compassionate, and unjudging. How to find balance and confidence, and the wisdom to offer light out into the world and feel it reflected back. How to reach out to others in ways that create meaningful connection.

And most of all, how to let love in and how to share it without reservation. Without applying any test of my worthiness, they have unfailingly offered me their companionship and their love. Through this purity of connection, they have brought forth from me the foundational qualities of the heart, tools that I have used to bushwhack my way to happiness, to cut through the debris and brambles my mind tosses in my way.

Nearly every morning, I sit on the floor in the dark, my eyes closed, drawing upon thoughts and images that slow my panicked chipmunk of a mind. Each morning, I call to mind a scene so familiar to me now, it's as if I have been there. My dogs and I are gathered at the edge of a large open field, tall brown grass stretching out in open invitation, a mountain beckoning to us, its rocky peak strong and sure against the wide blue sky. We are all there. Pal, his stub tail quivering with delight. Yankee, all long ears, and big paws, forever My Puppy. Took, nose down, smelling rabbits, ready to run, to share his joy. Buddy, freed from his cage and his itching, eyes on the edge of the field where the woods begin, one paw up in classic pointer pose. Gizmo, healed and happy, his red coat thick and shining, his face alight, just as in my dad's picture of him. Willie, lustrous black fur glowing in the low autumn sun, prancing with excitement, his eyes on mine, seeking his work with me. Jasper, little JJ, sitting calmly with the assurance of someone who's always felt in charge of how his life unfolded. Isabel, heart strong, her gaze locked on mine, telling me she will follow me anywhere. Gracie, moonbeam coat soft against the tawny grasses, her eyes also on mine, questioning. *I'm here*, she says. *Take me where you are going, and I will be by your side.* And Leo, his majestic head held tall on his strong neck, his nose quivering with the scents, his gaze shifting to me, soft, earnest, his wild, loving spirit penetrating mine. We are gathered under the angled rays of an early fall morning, at ease but also in shivering expectation. And then suddenly, there it is, a silent call, and we all begin to run through the grass reaching above my ankles, the dogs bounding and bouncing, our faces loose with joy. My dogs all around me, running, running with me to the mountain.

Notes

1. Boorstein, Sylvia. *Pay Attention, for Goodness' Sake: Practicing the Perfections of the Heart — The Buddhist Path of Kindness.* NY: Ballantine Books, 2002. pp. 79-80.
2. Boorstein, p. 163.
3. The Temple Buddhist Center: kshanti paramita: the perfection of patience" by Victor Dougherty. https://www.templebuddhistcenter.com/articles-mini-lessons/kshanti-paramita-the-perfection-of-patience.
4. BBC guide: The Dhamma in Buddhism: Six Perfections – Mahayana Buddhism. https://www.bbc.co.uk/bitesize/guides/zvw9dxs/revision/4.
5. Boorstein, p. 227.

Acknowledgements

This book came into being through the support of so many wonderful, caring people. My burning desire to share these stories could not have been realized without their wisdom, generosity, support, and loving kindness. My gratitude to all of them overflows.

Judy Bolton-Fasman and Julia Phillip led me to two talented teachers who shared essential guidance and helped me understand how to shape my memories into stories: Elissa Altman and David Berner. I am particularly indebted to David, who believed in this book from the beginning, helped me shape it with abundant gentleness, and then then led me to Amanda C. at Fiverr, who caught all my errors.

I am eternally grateful for the generous support of dear friends. Susanne cheered me on from the start. Kate, Kathleen, and Cherie offered to read the manuscript, and their warm responses, at a very vulnerable point, were essential to its fruition. Judy offered trusted guidance and genuine enthusiasm that got me started, and then clear-minded wisdom and loving support that took me across the finish line. June and I shared a year of studying the Ten Perfections through rich and joyful conversations that shaped my thoughts about these powerful teachings. Our study became the lens to see how my dogs have enriched my life.

Syliva Boorstein's book about The Ten Perfections, *Pay Attention for Goodness' Sake*, formed the basis of my understanding and appreciation of the heart qualities, and I am deeply and forever grateful for her wise, authentic, practical, and compassionate teachings, and for her encouragement when I told her about this book.

I also want to acknowledge the essential role of Dog B.O.N.E.S: Therapy Dogs of Massachusetts and its President and Founder, Jeanne Brouillette. Her leadership of this loving community of therapy dog teams has enriched my life beyond measure, bringing connection, joy, understanding—and so much fun. I am deeply and forever grateful.

At the heart of it all, through the many ups and downs, my partner Jaime was there, believing I could write a book—this book—even when I didn't. Jaime—whose very first text to me asked if I was a writer—never stopped believing. Through his believing, the impossible became possible.

About the Author

A retired librarian, Ellen now focuses on two lifelong passions: dogs and writing. She has decades of experience as a therapy dog volunteer and instructor with Dog B.O.N.E.S: Therapy Dogs of Massachusetts, and has been certified as a dog trainer and as a Certified Animal Assisted Intervention Specialist. She currently shares her life with two Golden Retrievers, Gracie and Leo, both certified therapy dogs. She and Leo volunteer at an elementary school as a therapy dog team.